J AMES R AMOS

Published by: RAMOS

MOVE WITH ME

by James Ramos

ISBN #978-0-9982239-4-0

Edited by Eli Gonzalez and Joe Wisinski

Book design by Debbie Bishop
Illustrations by Nathan Rodriguez

For information address inquiries to:

RAMOS

www.jamesramos.com

www.MoveWithMe.today

Printed in USA

DEDICATION

I want to dedicate this book to the two most influential women in my life:

My mother Mary Jane and my wife Connie.

I owe everything to you.

I am humbled by the love and kindness you have given me and all whom you touch. The generosity and selflessness that you display on a day-to-day basis is simply my most cherished gift that God has blessed on me. I only wish that my children possess your attributes. And no matter what —if they do— I am success.

You have molded me into who I am today.

Thank you and I love you with all my heart.

Your devoted son and husband, james.

TABLE OF CONTENTS

FOREWORD

I first met James Ramos when I was a Vice President for RE/MAX and one of the states under my direct supervision was Florida. I liked him right off the bat. He had a calm, reassuring energy about him but more importantly, after some small talk I could sense that he was driven to do great things - I love people in RE/MAX who are driven to do great things. It didn't hurt that he had an MBA and was fresh out of a stellar career with PepsiCo, a worldwide brand, just like RE/MAX.

In fact, I was so impressed with him and his vision that I set up a quick 30-minute meet and greet with Dave Liniger, the CEO and Co-Founder of RE/MAX. Like me, Dave took an instant liking to James and the 30-minute conversation grew to a three-hour conversation, with Dave sharing as much information he could to help James get started on the right track.

Well, James took the Tampa Bay area by storm. I've spoken with countless brokers about their ideas and plans but James dove right into execution. His agents will tell you that he's built the perfect brokerage for them and their market.

RE/MAX is in the people business. As the franchisor, our primary focus needs to be on the broker, the ones who purchased the franchise. We work diligently to increase profitability for them. In turn, we rely on our brokers to make their agents profitable and provide them world class service. It's on the broker to utilize RE/MAX, one of the top franchise brands in the world. Not many brokers in Real Estate can do that the way James has and will continue to do going forward.

There is a lot of downward pressure on the profitability in real estate right now. The consumer wants more for less, they want more value from the agent but want to pay him or her less. The agent wants more service from the broker but wants to pay less. It is up to the brokers to maximize their value for their agents. James is an expert at that. He's a cultivator of value.

I've learned quite a few truths during my career and here is one of them: people who are serious act like it. They throw the gauntlet down. Their mindset is to wake up every day to be the very best that day. This is a trait of those that provide immense value — all the time — in their business, and adapt to the changing challenges easily.

Dave Liniger put it best when he said, "If you do business today the way you did it yesterday, you'll be out of business tomorrow."

James has thrown the gauntlet down and put the Tampa Bay area on notice. "Either you move with me and keep up, or I'll leave you behind."

His innovations in this area, such as opening a coffee shop in downtown Tampa, and starting many other businesses that are all thoughtfully crafted, are designed for one purpose – to give his agents the edge in their marketplace and provide immense value to the consumer.

It's a dog-eat-dog world in real estate. I recommend you read this book and decide if you should align yourself with someone who wakes up every day to fight for his agents. I can't recommend this book, *Move With Me*, enough. Partly because it's a great book, but moreso because I have full confidence in the man who wrote it.

Adam Contos
Chief Operating Officer
RE/MAX

INTRODUCTION

The center of all I do is to bring families together, or as I often say, bring families back to the table. Most families, mine included, have wonderful memories where they gather to eat and share. A house is just a house, but a home... that's a special place. The kitchen table is the hub of a home. That's where, not only families share time together, but also where extended families such as aunts, uncles, cousins, and grandparents sit and talk. It's also where best friends talk to parents during sleepovers, where important conversations take place, where the mail is read, and where mom's cooking is shared and her legend begins to spread. Make no mistake about it; the kitchen table area is sacred ground... and I protect it.

By title, I suppose I own a real estate brokerage. But that's not who I am. I actually own several businesses, but that's not who I am either. Who I am is a husband, father, and son, first and foremost. In my businesses, I'm a Servant Leader.

I love what I do. In particular, I love helping my real estate agents.

I help agents to assist their clients in the most efficient, ethical, and practical ways possible. No other broker has built what I've built. Today's brokers don't support their agents the way my organization does. I say that with humility, but also with a sense of satisfaction because what my agents and associates accomplish, by putting people in homes they can afford, actually helps families stay together.

I'm honored to have more than 100 full-time professionals working in my various companies. Creating an entity that supports the success of that many people is a grave responsibility, especially when you consider their spouses and children. I don't take it for granted that they willingly signed up to work with me. To their surprise, they find out that it's not them who work for me; it is me who works for them. With me being 100 percent committed to them they will have the best chance to surpass the goals they've set for themselves.

Whenever I see one of my clients' kids go to college, or win an award, or I see pictures of them enjoying a family vacation; it reaffirms to me that I've built my brokerage and other businesses the right way. Sure, the way I do things is different. Actually, my brokerage is the only one of its kind. But that's what happens when you understand the future of an industry, you become a thought leader, an innovator.

My family has been in the real estate arena, specifically in construction, since 1956. You can say that I grew up with it. However, after graduating from the University of Florida with an Economics degree, I didn't follow the family path. I went to work for some of the largest consumer packaged goods manufacturers in the world. I worked for General Mills, Unilever, and PepsiCo; companies that manufacture and manage some of America's most famous brands.

In my various roles at those companies I had the opportunity to manage billion-dollar brands and billion-dollar customers. I worked in the amazing consumer goods industry for 18 years and learned from some of the best trainers in the world. During that time I was granted the opportunity to attend the Goizueta Business School at Emory University and received a masters in business administration, graduating with honors, thanks to General Mills. When I turned 40, after being promoted throughout the ranks in these global companies I found myself at a point where the organization was unable to develop me fast enough and offer experiences at the rate I desired, so I switched gears and focused on the single biggest consumer packaged good a family will invest in — homes.

I must say all evidence suggests that I'm on to something! In the five years that I've been in business, we have been responsible for more than $750 million in residential and development deals. We have had more than 3,000 transactions in our first five years. We have won 10 National Aurora Awards for stand out kitchen & bath design/build projects. We have been instrumental in countless families finding their dream home. We have supported our agents and associates in surpassing financial goals they never expected to. But what's most gratifying to me is that we have brought many families back to the kitchen table.

I wrote this book to wake up the real estate world. I have a message for you — you've been on cruise control for long enough! Let's have fun!

Everyone is stuck doing the same things. Brokers are offering the same stale services they've been offering for decades. Realtors® are still having to do everything on their own — find the lead, wash the lead, convert it to a referral, list the property in MLS, depend on outside parties to resolve improvement concerns that are needed for a property to sell, and be mired with details from contract to close. All the while, being that we are in the Information Age, year after year, do-it-yourselfer's are listing and selling their homes at a growing rate.

THIS BOOK IS FOR THREE GROUPS OF PEOPLE:

Group 1: People that are currently real estate agents. It is time for you to demand more from your broker. I'll explain how their lack of support, even if you don't think so yet, is holding you back.

Group 2: Intelligent go-getters that are tired of working for someone else and feel they would do well as a real estate agent. I'll show you an easier way to navigate the muddied waters of real estate and help you stand out from the crowd.

Group 3: Brokers. I actively consult brokers on doing

business wisely in the Information Age. There's a refreshing new twist happening and, although it's centered on the agents, you win big too! When your agents are best supported, you all win.

There's a better, smarter way to do business today. It's buoyed by collaboration, support, and different verticals working for the same cause. I'm excited for you to find out what I've built. I think you're going to love it. Agents have been feeding off just the buying and selling transactions for far too long. It's time to broaden your horizons.

If you're an agent, I think you're going to start having fun again. If you're considering the industry, the fun is about to start! I'm excited for you to discover the Ramos Way.

CHAPTER 1

THE WONDERFUL WORLD OF REAL ESTATE

Out with the Old, In with the New

If you've been a real estate agent for a long time, regardless of how successful you may have been, you might disagree with much of what I say and I'll tell you why...

This book isn't your typical book for Realtors® on how to buy and sell houses, how to set up an open house, how to stage a property, or how to realize when a client is giving you buying signals. Those books are outdated and boring. You shouldn't have to read a book to figure that stuff out.

This book is about the new way of being successful in real estate, about the future. You may disagree with what I have to say because you may be stuck in your ways. They've worked for you in the past so you continue to work for the same brokers and do the same things. But ready or not, agree with me or not, the methods for being a successful Realtor® have just changed and I'm here to show you how. I ask that you hold your judgment until you've read my methodology. Trust me, you'll be happy you did.

Personally, I love real estate. It's been good to me. The reason why I'm so passionate about what I do is because my most precious memories growing up revolved around our kitchen table. I grew up in a large family; I was the youngest of five boys. Yet, we had a 15-foot table right off the kitchen. My parents prepared a place where our extended family, my aunts, uncles, grandparents, cousins, and friends were always welcomed. It seemed that regardless of the day of the week, everyone wanted to be at our house for dinner. My parents also hosted the biggest holiday parties year after year. Many people remember that 15-foot kitchen table fondly.

As I became an adult I came to know exactly why my parents had a kitchen table that could seat more than our family of seven. They wanted us to grow up with love and laughter and that's exactly what surrounded our kitchen table. They created a home. I believe the single largest investment one can make for their family is to turn a house into a home, and a kitchen table is the epicenter of all that, regardless of its size. I'm proud to say that today I help bring families back to the table.

I'd like to pay homage to one of the oldest industries in the civilized era, buying and selling a home or property. It's a wonderful industry. You don't have to spend tens of thousands of dollars and give up four years of your life at a major university to get into this respected career. The best thing about it is that, although it will go through crashes, bursting bubbles, and droughts, buying a home will never go out of style.
However, the industry, amid so many technological

advances, still has an archaic rhythm to it. For centuries, not much has changed.

Sure, the industry got a shot of adrenaline when the Internet made information much more accessible. But still, even with easier ways to get leads and the ability to acquire knowledge through blogs and other informative websites that answer your questions with a swipe of a finger, real estate is still about selling a home for someone and helping someone else buy one.

FOLLOW THE MONEY

Real estate has always excited me. Every time someone buys a new home, there is a thrill not commonly seen when other purchases are made. When the agent hands a new homeowner the keys to his or her new house, it's a special moment. Everyone is full of smiles and often there are even some I-can't-believe-I-bought-a-house tears. Most homeowners still remember exactly where they were the first time they held the keys to their first house. It's a great feeling for the Realtor® as well, which is why it's one of the reasons people like being Realtors®. We all have an innate desire to help others and this profession grants us that. However, it's not the biggest reason. The ability to make a ton of money, that's the big draw.

For a Realtor®, there's no ceiling on how much one can make; this is one of the true cases where there literally isn't a cap on your earnings. At times the checks may be few and far between, but they're always big! That's why there are so many Realtors® out there; they're following the money, big money at that. In fact, the United States just added two new billionaires to the long list of people who accrued an incredible amount of wealth from real estate. David Walentas debuted on the billionaire's list with a net worth of $1.7 billion. And Jeff Sutton, the Manhattan retail landlord who brought American Girl to Fifth Avenue, commands some of the highest rents in the country. Sutton has a net worth of $2.7 billion. Like I said, big money.

The problem with the real estate industry, in terms of how Realtors® operate, is that many still think that their job is only about assisting others in buying or selling a home. They have the same mindset as house sellers had centuries ago. Now, many people make a good living at it that way, but that way of thinking is too narrow. If you want the opportunity to make the type of money that can help your future generations, you have to think bigger than buying and selling. It's time to expand your way of thinking. If you only feed from only one slice of the real estate pie, the odds will continually be stacked against you from accruing real wealth.

HOW I GOT INTO REAL ESTATE

I was an athlete growing up. I was one of those kids who had a knack for just about every sport I played. During my teenage years I began to focus on baseball and got pretty good at it. When I graduated from high school I was offered a baseball scholarship to the University of Florida. I learned more than I ever thought I would at college. Part of my learning came from what was taught in the classrooms, but much of it came from playing baseball and competing at a high level also. I graduated from UF with an Economics degree and went out to take the world by storm.

My official career began when I got hired at General Mills in 1993 as a sales representative. I worked in the consumer packaged goods (CPG) industry in sales and marketing roles from 1993 — 2011 with major companies such as General Mills, Unilever, and PepsiCo.

When I entered the industry, there were people who had worked there for decades. One particular person, who was a mentor to me when I first started, would say, "This job used to be all about relationships. I knew who to call, I knew what they wanted from me and, heck, I even knew some of their families. It was all about relationships." Then he would shake his head in dismay, "Not anymore. Now it's about shelf space, data, and inventory."

I respected him too much to be crass, so I never told him what I wanted to: It's all about economics.

He was right about one thing though; the industry was rapidly changing. The bottom line was that if your consumer goods were not selling, the retail store was not going to reorder. Or worse, they would make the company take the goods back, ultimately losing valuable real estate on a retailer's shelf.

As I was working, always rooted in roles that involved a high level of analytics, massive retailers started to consolidate their buying headquarters. No longer could you sell to regional offices, allowing you to build rapport with the buyers. Sellers of consumer packaged goods could only call on corporate headquarters. With fewer buyers, thus fewer points of contact, most companies didn't need as many salespeople. Relationship selling morphed into fact-based solution selling. The stories no longer mattered, the excuses were no longer accepted, and the mistakes were no longer tolerated. Only the performance of the product mattered.

After getting my feet wet and gaining valuable experience, I began to excel in every position I was put in. Working for major companies in managerial and analytical roles allowed me to understand not just my role, but also the big picture in terms of how each company fit within the vast world of corporate products in retail locations all over the world. One of the things that helped me in a very competitive industry is that, as a former D-1 athlete, I knew what it took to compete. I knew better than most the importance of taking the time to prepare in order to perform at an optimal level. While some of the roles were different, competition was never new to me.

My experiences helped me learn that there was a big difference between a competency and a skill. I also understood the many different functional roles that play a part in a global product and service organization. Part of the reason why I was so successful was, while other managers focused on their jobs and their numbers, as I did, I also understood the inner workings, the many moving parts of the industry. One of the other things I realized was how important a company's culture plays in its success. To have the right people, with the right mindset, in jobs tailored to their personalities, is critical for the growth and profitability of a company.

I had married my high school sweetheart in December of 1993. Luckily for us, she was a registered nurse. I say that because my career, either through promotion or downsizing, forced us to move 18 times in 23 years, so she was always able to land on her feet and get a job, regardless of where we moved. Somewhere during all of those moves, which included six rentals, nine homes I had to renovate, two I built from the ground up, and one that was move-in ready, I learned a lot about real estate. I learned more than many Realtors®.

But the real estate industry I learned was different than the type of real estate Realtors® are taught. Moving 18 times, going through the buying and selling processes as often as I did as a customer, building the homes, and working with a myriad of different laborers and tradesmen, gave me a perspective on real estate that excited me because I knew I could leverage it.

The more I moved, the more I believed that the Realtors® we used didn't see the big picture the way I did. They didn't discuss with me the many aspects of buying a home, such as design, furnishing, building, renovating, and landscaping. They would just talk to me about whether I liked the house, the square footage, and the neighborhood, the same way most do today. At first I thought some Realtors® were incompetent, but I quickly learned that it wasn't any one Realtor® in particular, most in the field was, and still is, short-sighted due to a lack of support and vision by their brokerage.

But what really excited me was when I realized that throughout all our moves we had made almost as much money as I had working for major companies in corporate America! I began to focus on becoming a Realtor® to see if I could build a career in real estate. Then in one defining moment, although it took moving 18 times and years of careful study, I realized that the real estate industry had to change for Realtors® and brokers to survive.

As my mentor all those years ago lamented to me, I foresaw many Realtors® complain that the way they used to do business wasn't working as effectively anymore. After having conversations with Realtors® and brokerage owners regarding my epiphany, I figured out something that really got my heart racing — No one else I spoke to knows the change that's about to overtake real estate, no one but me!

For many years, my wife and I had been having a conversation about the possibility of me going into real estate full time. I had never wanted to leave my cushy corporate job that provided us with a steady paycheck before, but the opportunity I saw was just too big to dismiss. Besides, I was tired of making a ton of money for the large corporations I worked for. I had learned much about the world of consumer goods, managing some of the largest brands in the world, but it was time for me to get into the largest consumer packaged most people would ever buy — property.

I had always wanted to control my own destiny, as most people do. There's so much power in that. The vision I saw for my company was crystalizing in my mind and, although I knew it would take a lot of work and that I would have to listen to a lot of "why are you doing that?" from people that didn't understand my vision, the time had come.

I remember having that final conversation with my wife about my career change. She had asked me, "Are you sure you want to get into real estate full time?"

I had answered, "I'm not getting into real estate, my love, I'm going to change it!"

CHAPTER 2

THE BIG PICTURE

It's easy to see an entire forest from 10,000 feet in the air. However, when you're on the ground, all you see are the trees around you. Thus, the overused and often misused expression, you can't see the forest for the trees. Basically, it means that one can't see the totality of a problem or situation because he or she is too involved in the details. In my experience, when it comes to being ultra successful in real estate, most Realtors® and brokers can't see the forest for the trees.

Realtors® are constantly chasing leads, networking, staging homes, and doing everything that every other Realtor® is doing. They all say that they're different, that they're unique, but in reality they're not. They're all offering the same thing. On the management side, brokers are trying to figure out ways to recruit and retain excellent talent. Some pay for leads and do everything else that every other broker does, and because of that, many have yet to experience the success they desire for themselves and their agents. The problem is that they have yet to see the big picture, the future.

Once I say what I'm about to say, you might nod and think, *I knew that.* However, I would call you out on it because if you never acted on it, knowing the benefits that came with it, you never knew it. It's beautiful in its simplicity, yet there is a lot of hard work to do this. Here it is. Are you ready? This bit of information will shift your mindset when it comes to real estate — if you want to become an ultra-successful broker of the future, you need to create more services for your Realtors®. If you want to become an ultra-successful Realtor®, you need to find a broker with the capacity to equip you to make money in more areas than just the transactions of buying or selling.

Did it not get you as excited as you had hoped? That could be because you still don't fully understand it. It's one thing to see the whole forest, but another thing altogether to understand how to extract the riches from it. It will all be explained in minute detail as you continue to read this book.

Everyone is busy trying to dominate the market, trying to own his or her backyard, but that's the old way of thinking when it comes to the future of real estate. I know this is contrary to everything you've learned since you were a child, but hear me out.

You don't have to dominate one area to make an incredible living. Even if you are the best at helping people buy or sell their home, you're still only getting paid from one or two pieces of the pie. You can make an incredible living by making money from every piece of the pie, from every transaction that goes with the totality of buying and selling homes. No one is doing that right now! But to do that, you have to know what you're made of.

WHAT ARE YOU MADE OF

You must be willing to step out on a limb, work more than you expected, miss out on some of life's pleasures, and work your tail off to be great. You need to have an inner drive that fuels your core beliefs and produces a vision of your best self, and you need to have the tenacity to endure setbacks to get there.

I believe that everyone has a level of greatness he or she can achieve. There have been people born with physical handicaps who, metaphorically and physically, have climbed mountains. Doctors have told some that they would never walk again or that they had six months to live, only to see them run a marathon three years later. The stories of Henry Ford, Walt Disney, and Oprah Winfrey have the narrative of almost giving up, of thinking that they should quit because of setback after setback, yet you know their names and know what they've accomplished.

Henry Ford — his first automobile company ended in bankruptcy, leaving him penniless, as did his second. He actually went completely broke five times.

Walt Disney — at the age of 22 he had to file for bankruptcy after the failure of a cartoon series in Kansas City. He traveled to Los Angeles with $40 in cash and an imitation leather suitcase that contained one shirt, two undershorts, two pairs of socks, and some drawing material.

Oprah Winfrey — she was fired from her first television job as a news anchor in Baltimore. They told her she would never make it because she was too emotional.

There are single mothers who wake up every day and fight on, working and parenting. With everything seemingly against them they're raising respectful young men and women. People that never graduated high school have become millionaires. The four-minute mile has been shattered, humans have traveled to the moon, and the Chicago Cubs won a World Series. Many people throughout centuries have obtained what others once thought was impossible. You may not know all the great stories about overcoming adversity from everyone who has done so, and that's okay, you don't have to. You just need to have the conviction and perseverance to write your own.

Here's some truth for you; I can give you the blueprint to be ultra successful, but if you don't own it, if you can't envision seeing yourself like that, if you don't embrace that philosophical change has come to the world of real estate, you're not going to capitalize on it.

THE PRESENT

Before I discuss the future of real estate, first let's come to the same level of understanding on the present. The National Association of Realtors® has the most updated statistics on the industry. This is the organization that requires people to put the trademark R, "®" every time someone writes down the words Realtors® and Realtor®.

Here are some statistics I found on their site that I think you're going to find interesting:

- There are about two million active real estate licenses in the United States, according to the Association of Real Estate License Law Officials (ARELLO)

- 62 percent of all Realtors® are female and the median age is 58

- The typical Realtor® is a 53-year-old white female homeowner with some college education

- The median gross income of Realtors® was $39,200 in 2015, down from $45,800 in 2014

- FSBOs (For Sale By Owner) accounted for 8 percent of home sales in 2015

- The typical home sold by FSBOs was $185,000

- The typical home sold with assistance from an agent was $240,000

Since I'm mentioning The National Association of Realtors®, do you know the difference between a real estate agent and a Realtor®? Although both are licensed to sell real estate, they are not the same. The main difference between the two is that a Realtor® is a member of the National Association of Realtors®. That means that he or she must subscribe to the Realtor® Code of Ethics; made up of 17 Articles and more than 80 detailed Standards of

Practice. This matters to many consumers.

Here's what TheBalance.com has to say about it:
The Code of Ethics is strictly enforced by local real estate boards. The 17 Articles of the Code of Ethics also contains various underlying Standards of Practice. It's not just a bunch of rules that agents swear to uphold and adhere to because their broker made them join the Board. The Standards are much more restrictive and confining to conduct than those state guidelines governing agents who simply hold a real estate license.

While there is no evidence nor guarantee that all REALTORS® are morally or ethically better than unaffiliated real estate agents, it is an attempt by the industry to regulate and, as such, deserves recognition.

Personally, I like having Realtors® working at RE/MAX Bay to Bay. I am driven by a moral compass and live and play by my core values, so those that allow themselves to be subjected to a higher level of standard are people I like to work with. At the core of it all though, are the agents. So for the remainder of this book, I'll forego adding that little trademark R and just write "agent" because it describes everyone that helps buyers buy a home and sellers sell a home.

Every agent has been affected by a growing phenomenon — un-licensed owners selling their own homes. They are commonly referred within the industry as FSBO's (pronounced *fizboze*), which comes from the popular sign — For Sale By Owner. Seemingly against reason and profit margin, FSBO's are becoming more and more common.

This is despite the fact that a home seller will make more of a profit (up to 28 percent more) by using an agent, even after his or her fee has been collected.

The reason why FSBO's are growing is because of all of the information available. What used to be only privy to agents is now, for the most part, available to anyone. People not formally trained or educated on real estate now feel equipped to buy or sell a home without the assistance of a trained professional. Agents find themselves at a disadvantage when they can't articulate clear points of differentiation in terms of marketing a home to homeowners. This causes many agents to lose their credibility, thus the listing, and the homeowner makes less of a profit when the house is sold. This is a classic lose/lose scenario.

Yet, brokerage firms today aren't equipping their agents to have a solution in their bag for every concern raised by a potential client. Worse still is that many agents haven't even considered asking for more help. They simply don't know what they don't know.

If the rate of FSBOs continues to increase, the future for real estate agents and brokers is bleak. The question then becomes, how can we stop the growth of FSBOs if these sellers think they have as much or more information and resources than we do?

Let me introduce you to the methodology of Gen. Stan McChrystal.

MODERN WARFARE

I first saw McChrystal at the MGM Grand Resort and

Casino in Las Vegas. He was a featured speaker at R4, RE/MAX's annual international convention, hosted by Jay Leno. He took the stage on a Wednesday morning and pretty much put into words the changes and patterns I felt were needed in the real estate industry. I was amazed as he articulated how the modern battlefield could teach the modern business world, much in the way Sun Tzu did with his book, *The Art of War.*

Before I share with you the methods of his madness, first let me properly introduce you to a man who should go down as an American Hero. Stanley Allen McChrystal is a retired United States Army general. He is best known for his command of Joint Special Operations Command (JSOC) in the mid 2000's. His last assignment was as Commander, International Security Assistance Force (ISAF) Commander, U.S. Forces Afghanistan. He was credited with the death of Abu Musab as-Zarqawi, leader of Al-Qaeda in Iraq. He was known for saying and thinking what other military leaders were afraid to.

After retiring from the military, along with becoming involved with many organizations, he established a consultancy firm in 2011 called McChrystal Group. They use the slogan "Bringing Lessons from the Battlefield to the Boardroom." And that's what he spoke about that morning.

In his speech, he relayed the biggest problem the United States and its allies were having with their war against Al-Qaeda. They were trying to fight an enemy like they would fight themselves, by killing off their leaders. However, the problem was that Al-Qaeda was not set up organizationally or structurally like the United States or former enemies of the United States. I was riveted. After his speech, I looked up information on him and the compelling story he shared and found an article he published on June 21, 2013 on LinkedIn.

We desperately wanted Al Qaeda in Iraq to be organized like we were, so that we could understand it, analyze it, pick it apart, and, ultimately, defeat it. Remove the leadership, some believed, and the organization would crumble.

But they hadn't taken into account that they were fighting a different type of enemy. We had brought an industrial age force to an information age conflict.

See, our military, like our business models, starts at the top with a CEO type. Then it goes to executives and managers. Every level you go down, the more people there are.

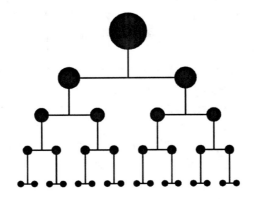

However, the Al-Qaeda organization, made up of complex social, familial, tribal, and marital ties, looked more like this:

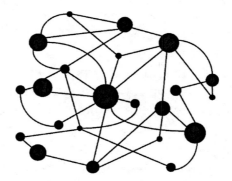

With the two images staring at us — one clean, crisp, and familiar; the other random, seemingly chaotic, and alien — I offered a thought to summarize the discussion we'd been having for several weeks. "In this fight, we are not facing an organized army. We all agree that with that structure," pointing to our standard hierarchical model, "we can outmaneuver any army in the world — but that's not our challenge here. We need to be able to outmaneuver a network. Our structure can't do that."

I want you to think about the real estate industry as the battleground as you continue to read this section. Brokers still have the Industrial Age mentality to win the "war," but to make the most money, they need to modernize their way of thinking and utilize the tools in the Information Age to equip the agents with more tools.

McChrystal then went on to say, "If we are going to win, we need to become a network."

Shortly after that discussion, a Naval officer said, "Sir, you can't steer something that isn't moving."

So they did just that. They started to move and create a new network to take on an enemy from the Information Age. Constant change became the hallmark of his task force. Each node, each small team, had to be fully equipped to defeat the enemies' small teams.

We'd also realized that as small 2- or 3-person elements had become hyper-empowered in the information age, it made our networked approach all the more necessary.

Even small teams of Al Qaeda insurgents in distant, dusty corners of Iraq could access and share information globally, and in near real time. Through posting grisly videos of their suicide bombings online, for example, they magnified their actions in the eyes of the world audience, drummed up recruits and donations from sympathetic spectators, and made themselves all the more terrifying to Iraqis. This power for individuals and small groups to be suddenly, powerfully disruptive was a third dimension of complexity — and is a new variable facing many of today's industries.

Are you getting a glimpse into what the future of real estate is about? I'll explain it plainly for you.

FUTURE

The traditional hierarchical organizational charts presently in brokerage firms do not adequately capture the best ways to equip an agent in the 21st century. Information is moving faster than ever before. People looking to buy or sell a home at times are better equipped with information and contacts. They can also make better long-term plans, which is creating a vortex, a black hole, if you will, that is slowly swallowing up dollars from agents and thus impacting brokers in a big way.

Agents of the near future will no longer be able to compete if they can't offer a one-stop-shop service. They need to be able to provide solutions for homebuyers and sellers not only in the buying or selling process, but also in the design, building, and furnishing aspects of home buying.

When you consider the totality of buying a home, take that 10,000-feet view of it, you'll see that there are so many spokes in the massive wheel that make it go around.

Here are some activities a homebuyer will spend money on when purchasing a home:

- The land and the home

- A commission to the agent, if one was used

- A title agent and/or attorney to close and record the deal

- A mortgage banker if it is not a cash transaction

- An insurance broker to purchase hazard insurance, and in some cases, flood and wind coverage.
- A designer, a builder, sub-contractors

- The purchase and delivery of products to furnish the home.

- All the professionals who help maintain the home, including cleaning, pool care, landscaping, and so on.

There are more than 30 additional entities that come into play when any sort of renovation becomes a part of the home-buying effort. A simple renovation that starts with demolition and ends with landscaping may take dealing with subcontractors, vendors, designers, architects, city municipalities (for permits), plumbers, appliance stores, landscapers, and the list goes on.

One of the main reasons why agents don't delve too deeply into these areas is because of the complexity of these daunting tasks. Instead, they refer their clients to different tradesmen, and that's all they do in terms of providing additional service.

But, and here's where this gets really good, how about if there was a brokerage that had all of those components under the same umbrella? And how about if the agent was able to do more deals and offer a higher level of service in the home buying process?

Imagine how much money a real estate agent could make if he or she was equipped as a one-person network? Imagine if they knew the nuances of every facet of the house buying or selling process. He or she would own the information age!

Of course, for that to happen the agent would need to work for a forward-thinking broker that acquired or developed businesses that could professionally and expertly supply every demand.

That's exactly what I wanted to build. That was my vision. But before I could make my vision a reality, I needed a powerful ally. After careful consideration, I chose RE/MAX.

CHAPTER 3

RE/MAX LLC

Shopping for a franchise was an interesting journey for me. It forced me to really get in touch with who I am, my values, and how I want to be perceived. After all, buying a franchise is not the same as buying furniture or a car. You're hoping to commit yourself to it for the rest of your career. My family had been in real estate in one form or another for 61 years and we had taken great care to do what was right for our many clients. I had to ensure that I would protect the reputation that had taken my family a long time to establish. After all, it wasn't just me — James Ramos — who was going to align with a real estate franchise, it was the Ramos name. After much internal searching, I chose RE/MAX, and it wasn't even close.

Re/Max is number one in brand awareness. That was important to me. I was coming from working at PepsiCo, a heavy marketing company that built a brand known all around the world. I took a step back though and surveyed the market I would service, and to my delight the RE/MAX locations were low in comparison to the density they had in other major markets in the country. I researched markets that were similar to mine at one point, where RE/MAX had a smaller share of the business, and found that due to the company's marketing prowess and brokers with the same strategic intent of the RE/MAX philosophy they quickly eroded the competitors' share.

Then I considered the Tampa Bay area, one of the fastest growing real estate markets in the country, and I began to lick my chops. I thought, *Okay I can have the best branded real estate company backing me up in a market that's not saturated with locations, and that is also one of the fastest growing markets in the country?*

Then I met key management members at RE/MAX, LLC. I saw how they operated and found it to be similar to my great experiences in corporate America. I was sold!

I remember the day I opened in South Tampa. I was at a Starbucks and saw someone I knew, a fellow RE/MAX broker, or so I thought. It turned out that the very day I opened, he closed! I saw it as a great sign. More market share for the taking! I actually bought the franchise before I even had a broker. You may think I'm crazy, but I did a lot of research and I was thrilled with what I found about RE/MAX.

I'd like to give you a closer look at RE/MAX so you can see why I went with them. They truly are the best in their industry. Check out these statistics:

BRAND NAME AWARENESS — NUMBER ONE

As I've mentioned, before I started my brokerage I was at

some of the biggest consumer packaged goods companies in the world. Everyone everywhere knew our name. I mean, even people that don't drink Pepsi know Pepsi. Being trained at those companies by brilliant strategists on branding and knowing how to leverage instant recognition really taught me the true value of a brand. A brand isn't a company's colors, nor is it a logo. A brand is something identifiable. Just about every company, including the moms and pops, have a logo and maybe even some sort of color scheme that matches their brick and mortar location, their website, their business cards. Their logo may even be on hats. However, that does not mean that they have a brand.

A brand identifies you to people. If you think Pepsi, you might get an image of a glass of their soda with three or four ice cubes and you might even think of the fizzing on top of the glass that happens when a Pepsi has just been poured. Or, you might think of their logo. Regardless of what you think of, you can identify with the effects of the product just by its name. Forget about knowing a product by an image, that's what Fortune 5000 companies do. The top companies in the world know how to make you feel the sensation or effects of their product. That is branding.

Well, RE/MAX is number one in their industry in brand recognition! When someone sees a RE/MAX sign, they don't have to ask which company it is. They recognize it. Part of the reason, I think, is that RE/MAX isn't interested in part timers. They want brokers and agents who want to be the best. Ask any athlete who's made it to the pros if they didn't take their craft seriously enough to go full time in their preparation. It doesn't happen. Even the most gifted of athletes put 100 percent into their training to get to the level they are now. When I checked to see if RE/MAX was the company they claimed to be, I found my next reason to partner with them.

AGENTS AVERAGE YEARS — 15.4

That one really blew me away. It takes years for someone to become an expert in an industry. The fact that the average tenure of agents at RE/MAX is more than 15 years suggests to me that their agents must be good to be in the industry for so long. If the average tenure is 15 years, about half the agents there have worked for longer than that.

It spoke volumes to me because these people know what they're doing. They've been around the block a few times. It also told me that the agents that come to RE/MAX want to have long careers. Those are the types of people I want to attract; industry savvy people who are serious because they are in it for the long haul. I want people that don't have a Plan B.

U.S. HOME SALES — NUMBER ONE

No one sells more homes than RE/MAX. No one. I wasn't sure I needed any more convincing, but then I saw the stat that I liked the most.

AVERAGE COMMISSIONS OF RE/MAX AGENTS — $115,446.

I was blown away when I saw that. Earlier in this book, you may recall, I mentioned that the median income of Realtors

34

was $39,200 in 2015, well, the average RE/MAX agent nearly triples that!

I know some people who feel they had a great year if they made $80,000. I don't mean any disrespect to anyone who makes that kind of money because that's good money. But I'm going to call it like it is. That would be subpar for a RE/MAX agent. As I was considering RE/MAX, I was envisioning interviews I would have with potential agents. And when the conversation turned to money, as every interview conversation should, I believed I would come from a position of strength when I would say, "Well, I'm not building your average brokerage. With me you'll have many more services at your disposal than with any other brokerage. But so you know, the average RE/MAX agent makes more than $115,000 a year."

I can go on and on with why I chose RE/MAX but I'll stop with just those four points because, frankly, that was enough for me. However, nothing beat the time I went to my first RE/MAX International meeting in Las Vegas. It was epic.

MY VISIT WITH THE CEO AND CO-FOUNDER, DAVE LINIGER

I was speaking to Adam Contos, the gentleman who honored me immensely by writing the foreword for this book. He was the Senior VP of my region at the time. I was sharing with him my plans and asking a lot of questions to make sure I was doing things the right way. To my surprise, he asked me if I wanted to meet with Dave Liniger for a quick visit. Liniger is the CEO and co-founder of RE/MAX, the man whose vision and leadership grew RE/MAX to be the amazing brand it is. He and his wife founded the real estate franchise that was ranked number one for eight consecutive years. RE/MAX LLC is also in the top 10 of all the franchises in the world. It's actually ranked at number eight, a spot ahead of Wendy's and two spots ahead of Marriott Hotels & Resorts, which round out the top 10. Needless to say, I was very humbled about the opportunity.

I met with Adam at 10 a.m., as he suggested. We went up to Liniger's suite at the Mandalay Bay Resort and Casino. The elevator door opened to the largest hotel room I had ever seen. I was taken aback by how personable he was from the outset. He greeted me like an old friend. He asked me a lot of questions, not all of them about business. But when I started to share with him my ideas, the conversation really went into full swing.

I knew about many of his accomplishments, although much of his work happened many years ago, as Liniger is not a young man anymore. But I was amazed at how in touch and relevant his thoughts and ideas were. He is sharper now than I think ever before.

The 30 minutes came and went and I felt badly about taking more of his time than was originally offered to me, but I wasn't going to be the one to stop it. He stopped in mid-sentence, though, and glanced at his watch. I was sure my time with him was done.

"Hey, it's past our time," he said. Would you care to stay a little longer or do you need to be somewhere else?"

I was exactly where I needed to be. I was with Dave Liniger, who I have the utmost respect for, and Adam Contos, the Chief Operating Officer, who prior to that headed up the Florida region. Under his leadership, the Florida region was named Region of the Year in 2011 and 2012, before he was promoted in 2013. Dave's wife, Gail Liniger, was there as well. She is the Vice Chair and other co-founder. Gail is involved in day-to-day operations at RE/MAX Headquarters and knows as much about the company as anyone in the world. She was recognized as one of the top 10 U.S. women for her outstanding achievements in business, the arts, and public service. There were a few other high level executives there as well. There was no place else I needed to be.

Dave continued to share with me and I must say, while he's very dynamic in a conference setting, it pales to comparison to when he's speaking directly at you. During that time he told me an interesting story about another global brokerage that sued him for millions of dollars for stating RE/MAX was number one.

"Well, I knew they started a fight they couldn't win, so I went into it with guns blazing."

He told me how they expected him to not want to put up the amount of money it took to fight that type of legal battle, but they underestimated how important being number one was to him. He had worked too hard for it. He ultimately proved he was right, countersued, and won a huge victory.

By the time I left his penthouse, any bit of doubt had fled

my mind. I had just spent three hours with the man who revolutionized the industry and built the best brand in the industry, and I had just come on board. It spoke volumes to me as the type of leader he is. I can honestly say that his leadership has helped me to become the type of leader I am today.

I've benefited greatly from the RE/MAX name. As soon as I started my brokerage, a few very well-to-do agents who were working out of the RE/MAX brokerage that had closed came to me. In fact, my longest-tenured agents are other RE/MAX agents who trust the brand because it has done well by them. Lawrence Malloy was one of them.

Lawrence Malloy RE/MAX Bay to Bay Realtor®

"The RE/MAX office I was working out of was closing when James opened his. Back then the market was crashing, and it was hard to be innovative. But after James shared his vision with me, I quickly took up some office space for my assistant and I."

"It was important for me to stay with RE/MAX because of their brand recognition. Everyone knows who they are. Explaining the company that supports the brokerage is one less conversation I had to deal with."

CHAPTER 4

RE/MAX BAY TO BAY
AND RAMOS DESIGN BUILD

I had chosen the right brokerage, now I had to choose the right broker!

So I bought a brokerage but I didn't have a broker! Luckily for me, I found Zoe Green.

I had asked Paul, one of my brothers, if he knew of a really good broker, and he immediately mentioned, without thinking twice, Becky Eckley. Paul worked in mortgage at a RE/MAX brokerage where Becky was the broker. So I set up an appointment to meet Becky. When she came, she brought Zoe Green. Zoe had started as a receptionist working for Becky more than 20 years ago. I had the opportunity to interview both of them and was fortunate to get them both, Zoe as the broker and Becky as one of our first agents.

I'll let Zoe tell you the story of how she and I came to work together in her own words...

ZOE GREEN

I didn't want to do it.

I had delivered twins and was itching to get back into sales. But I was a broker for another company and the experience left a bad taste in my mouth, so when Paul called me and told me that his brother had bought a RE/MAX franchise, I was skeptical. Had it been anyone else, I would have politely turned down the offer, but because it was a Ramos and I knew Paul and his family's reputation, including James', I considered it, although it wasn't a high priority for me.

I met James and instantly could feel his energy. He told me of his vision and it was far more ambitious than anything I ever heard a broker say. Still, I had my reservations because when I was a broker the first time, the owner of the office was a selling broker, as was I. It was difficult to get the agents to trust you when you compete directly with them. When their leads get slow or if you have a hot streak, they wonder if you're cherry-picking the leads and things can get downright nasty. Things could get very competitive and people isolate themselves in those types of offices and don't work well with others. I didn't want any part of that type of environment again.

James said that was fine because that wasn't part of his plan anyway. He wanted me to be a non-selling, full-time manager. My main role would be to fully help the agents build their business. To get to know them, mentor those that needed mentoring, letting those people go that don't need handholding, and being there as a mentor and voice of reason for the many challenges they face. I was ecstatic when I heard the job description. I sought advice from close friends, people that know me well, and they encouraged me to take it. "You love helping people, building them up, you'll be playing to your strengths."

I accepted the position and I remember when we started I had a construction table and a laptop. We had zero agents. Since then, we've hired more than 150 agents. Not all of them were great fits, but many of them were and are doing very well today. We've grown to four locations and we offer more services and support than any other brokerage I've ever heard of.

I make it a point to get to know every agent who works with us. I do the onboarding, I get to know them as people, I inquire about their families, learn about their hobbies, and most of all, I help them create their unique business plans and business models. Other brokerages have staff that handle a lot of that but I do it because our agents are not just a number on a roster to me.

I'm excited about the future because James is such a thought leader. The coffee shop office concept is evidence of that. Millennials will soon be our fastest growing market. He realized that we need to be where they go, urban environments and coffee shops, so he bought a coffee shop in an urban environment; actually, he bought the brand so we can open more in the future!

I truly believe the sky is the limit because of what we've been able to accomplish in just five years. We have done our market research, our due diligence, if you will, and have built an incredible infrastructure capable of providing sensible resources and tools for the right agents. Now we are actively on the hunt for the best real estate agents we can find to band with the Ramos name, which is supported by the number one brand in the world. Yes, I'm very excited for our future. In fact, it's here now!

I'm incredibly proud of the results RE/MAX Bay to Bay has achieved in just five years. I wrote about the achievements we've accomplished in this book already, so I won't repeat them again, but I will say we have been so fortunate to work with such quality people that are so laser focused and dedicated to their success that I can't help but want to heap more praise on them.

I'm always on the move. Making plans and creating new paths is in the fabric of my DNA. I'll humbly say that I own a lot of businesses that have something to do with real estate. However, I won't mention them all here, although they are each extremely important and valuable to me. The one that started it all, though, is my construction company.

RAMOS DESIGN BUILD

I'm a licensed General Contractor. Among other things, that means I have in-depth, intimate knowledge of the entire construction process, from concept and design to the finished product, an elegant home. We focus on the high-end luxury home market. We have the ability to cater to a client who needs land, needs help with designing their home, constructing the home, and furnishing the home. The majority of our projects end up being homes valued at more than $1 million. I work hand in hand with excellent designers and architects so that we can take on ground up construction or renovations that deal with just a kitchen or renovations that involve an entire house, including an addition.

One of the main benefits of working with Ramos Build Design is that my clients have one point of contact to oversee everything. When clients work with multiple parties for home building projects and something goes wrong, there's a lot of finger-pointing. The architect might blame the designer, the contractor might point to the architect, and so on. It can get so convoluted that deadlines are blown by and the project exceeds the budget. And this all may have started in the first inning of pre-construction planning with a poor team. With me managing the entire process and my team handling it, things run much smoother.

There are many reasons why I think we've been as successful as we have but I'll only list two. The first is that we don't bid on projects. I think it has cost us a lot of potential business, but the reality of it is, we have built such a stellar reputation (and I hope I don't come across as being braggadocios), that our target market comes to us because of our name. We've been fortunate enough to be selected to work on several historical renovations in the area, which I believe is the best testament as to the type of name Ramos Design Build had earned. I fully stand behind our quality and craftsmanship, as do our clients.

Another thing that separates us is how we construct the shell of the home. What I mean by shell is the outside construction of a home, some are block, some are wood, and many are a combination of the two. I'm a representative of a company called Fox Blocks. We build our shells out of ICF – Insulated Concrete Forms. It's the best type of stability for any home because it's a poured solid wall that, at the center, has 6 to 10 inches of poured concrete. Some of the benefits of this is that it's rated to withstand winds of more than 200 miles per hour, there are no termite issues because it's not made of wood, and it's green, which means it drives down the efficiencies of a home. For example, a 5,000-square foot home we built has a monthly electric bill at less than $100.

The Ramos Design Build office is in the same location as RE/MAX Bay to Bay headquarters. As I've been saying, I have quite a few other entities in there to service our agents as well, such as Dakota and others. I'm excited to introduce you to them.

THE COOPERATIVE APPROACH

With the help of some very intelligent people and a very good team, I put together the brokerage of the future; an agent-centric model designed to enhance each agent's knowledge and offerings so they could grow faster and sell more.

STORE WITHIN A STORE

Having vetted and responsible vendors is great. However, it's even better if a select group of key professionals are a part of your organization, which is why I continue to build companies that can do the job from under the same roof. I utilize a concept similar to the one used by many forward-thinking verticals, called cooperative.

A Cooperative (Co-op) is an autonomous association of people united voluntarily to meet their common economic, social, and cultural needs and aspirations through a jointly owned and democratically controlled business. The co-op approach allows for various subcontractor and vendors to participate. And with Ramos managing the entity to ensure proper process and protocol is met it drives consistent service to the agents.

BENEFITS OF A CO-OP

Farmer's Cooperative Inc., (Farmer's Co-op) has been serving farmers ranchers, and gardeners in North Florida with everything from fertilizers, feeds, and farm supplies to residential LP gas since 1946. Their motto is "One Team, One Goal, Excellent Customer Service." The interesting thing about their motto is that they are actually made up of many companies. Although there are many different verticals in this co-op, they leverage their collective buying power and influence so that each member can benefit from it. This gives definition to the phrase, "the sum is greater than its parts."

The co-op term, though, is still relatively unknown. Co-operatives are a phenomenon taking hold right now in bigger cities, in particular in the commercial office space sector. In the world of brokers, co-op, the way I do it, is non-existent.

Basically, this is the co-op concept: smaller sized companies or entrepreneurs who can't afford prime retail or office space on their own partner up (or co-op) to share space with other similar sized companies. Typically, each company will provide a different service and cater to a different clientele. Each company receives the same benefits: great location, Wi-Fi, use of a kitchen, a commercial mailing address, access to conference rooms, printer access, an answering service, an administrative greeter, and more, depending on the space.

One of the benefits of working in one of these co-op spaces is that it exudes a sense of legitimacy for the renter. With more and more people working for themselves and working from home, people are seeking a more professional setting to work from than a Starbucks. Also, people working from home miss out on the energy, the flow of intelligent conversation from working alongside other professionals. I'm sure the conversations people have with their 8 year old are riveting, but they don't do much to get their professionally creative minds churning out new ideas.

They share the space the same way they do the rent. Now, instead of their business address being the same as their home address, they have a much more upscale location that lends them more credibility. It's a win/win, and I love win/wins.

I told you a little about me in the first chapter and about RE/MAX in the fourth; now let me tell you a little more about my organization:

- In a short period of time, five years, the Ramos family of companies is responsible for more than $750 million in residential sales and development deals.

- We have done more than 3,000 transactions in our first five years

- We have 100 full-time professionals who all pull their weight.

- We have won 10 national Aurora awards for Stand Out Kitchen & Bath Design as well as for Build Projects.

- The Ramos family name is synonymous with tens of thousands of successful residential and commercial construction projects in the southern United States dating back to 1956

Suffice it to say we know what we are doing. I've figured out that when most people buy a home, it's never how they want it when they get it. Unfortunately, many people settle for lesser quality than they wanted, pay more than expected, and have nightmare experiences working with laborers who usually never stick to a set timeline.

We solve those problems through our comprehensive line of services. I'm excited to share with you what makes Ramos stand apart from the crowded marketplace of brokers who continue to do the same things they've been doing for 20, 30, or 40 years. I believe you'll understand clearly why real estate agents love working here, and where the future of real estate is going.

I have established, in a first-class office space, a co-op style environment. However, instead of each vertical servicing a different industry, all the companies serve the same consumer, people looking to buy or sell a home. As I mentioned before, transacting with more than 30 entities takes place before a family is settled into a new home that may need a renovation.

I have taken the key elements of designing, building, and furnishing and have built different companies to service those areas. All those companies share space, which invites collaboration between the agents and the service providers they need to keep their clients satisfied.

Everything I do is with my agents' success in mind. Having all these companies under the same umbrella and incentivizing them to work with one another keeps our service at the highest of levels.

The future for brokers is in diversity. I have established different companies that intertwine with one another, giving my agents the best tools to be successful and giving our clients the best experience possible. I equip my agents with the resources that owners selling their own home and other agents don't have.

DAKOTA DESIGN BUILD COOPERATIVE

I formed a company called Dakota Design Build Cooperative. It was designed to cater to a group of multidisciplinary professionals with one common goal, to simplify Design, Build, and Furnish. We provide solutions for agents who require assistance in those areas.

It's a similar concept to the co-op model, but instead of it being solely for my agents, it's also for vendors and subcontractors. I have provided a place where people who specialize in design, build, and furnish can collaborate and help one another out, whether by giving expert advice or by taking on a job.

My construction company can't handle all of the business that all my agents bring us, so our approved vendors, general contractors, and subcontractors can find plenty of business there and the agents won't have to search far and wide for them. It also encourages our vendors to be more loyal to the Ramos brand, which further helps our agents. It's the perfect place for people who typically only deal with the buy and sell transactions of real estate (agents) to work with those who specialize in the design, build and furnish transactions of real estate (designers, architects, builders, and engineers) in a space that's conducive for all of them. Everybody wins at Dakota.

Each branch of this organization began as an independent business that naturally developed to help bridge the gap between the construction, design, and real estate worlds. Over time, Dakota has evolved into a collaborative entity that offers turnkey solutions for every phase, including designing, building, and furnishing. At Ramos, through Dakota, it all happens under one roof, thus eliminating confusion, saving time, and ensuring that all parties are on the same page.

Let me explain. Basically, I vertically integrated the most intimate items of construction, whether it is a renovation or a ground up project. Dakota specializes in the heart of every home, the kitchen. In particular, our focus is on cabinetry, countertops, and flooring. Dakota boasts a 5,000-square foot, state-of-the-art showroom. It's an interactive design center in a real estate office. It's a central location for contractors, designers, architects, engineers, and agents to best work together.

In the real world, and this happens all the time, a couple may love a house, but the wife wants to renovate the kitchen or it's a deal breaker. Or someone may want to get a certain amount for their home, but first he or she needs to upgrade the kitchen to make the house sellable.

Many agents want to scream when they hear the words, "I want to move forward, but before I do, I need… " The agent instantly sees his or her potential commissions running far, far away. They instantly realize that it's going to take a long time from contract to closing because now some sort of improvement has to happen. As any experienced agent knows, anybody can get a client to contract, but the rubber meets the road during the contract to close phase.

This means that now their client is going to undergo the daunting task of finding the right people for the right price with the right products that can do the right job in the right amount of time. So many things need to go right before the contract actually closes and the agent gets paid. The longer it takes, the more danger the agent faces of losing the deal.

Dakota helps shrink the time from list to contract and from contract to closing, allowing Ramos agents to get paid faster and giving them more opportunity to move onto servicing another customer.

My agents understand the process. Before the customer actually says the words, "renovation" they are prepared with a response. It goes something like this:

"I figured you'd say that and, quite frankly, I agree with you. Let's meet tomorrow at our showroom so that I can put a comprehensive plan in place for you to make this as easy for you as possible. We have the highest quality products of well-established name brands, in house, that I think you'll be interested in. We also have information on doors, windows, plumbing, and everything else associated in the type of project you want.

"Also, I can have a designer and a contractor meet with us to tell you what is or isn't possible. As an experienced team, we will brainstorm with you to get you the renovation you want at a price you're comfortable with. At the very least, you'll leave there with a comprehensive game plan on how to proceed."

How's that for service? Not many agents can say that to a customer. Most agents look at their contact lists and share the contact of a contractor and crosses their fingers. Would you rather have a renovation conversation at a Starbucks or in a cutting edge, up-to-date showroom?

DAKOTA KITCHEN & BATH

Of all the vendors we refer out, we refer most to Dakota Kitchen & Bath, a Ramos owned company. We chose to vertically integrate on kitchens and baths. This means a consumer who works with Ramos deals directly with the manufacturer, and there is no middle man. The reason we chose to own and operate this company is because we wanted to have our finger on the pulse of the most important part of the decision making process when it comes to improving a home. After all, the kitchen and master bath are what bring the most value to a home. In our showroom you will find high-end quality products. The type of products we have aligned with is indicative of the market we cater to in the Tampa Bay area.

For instance, I'm a manufacturer's representative for Bremtown Cabinetry, a company that specializes in high-quality, all-wood custom cabinetry and understands Florida design trends and the challenges of a "near-ocean" environment. I am also a representative for The Galley, which is an award-winning kitchen designer who invented highly engineered kitchen sinks, which are handcrafted in the USA. This unique sink can be built up to seven feet long. When a client likes the kitchen on display, they can purchase then and there. And as you know, every kitchen and bath requires a floor. We are manufacturers' reps for various hardwood, tile, and stone manufacturers. Being a manufacturers' rep for flooring, cabinetry and countertops offers our agents' customers choice and better value. It also saves them time and allows the process to move forward.

I've also formed strategic partnerships with companies I trust because I believe it is important to have direct connections with excellent manufacturers. We have resource guides on their products in our showrooms that we can show our customers. At times, these manufacturers will even come in our showroom to do events. We work closely with companies such as Kohler for plumbing fixtures, JELD-WEN for windows and doors, and Sub Zero and Wolf for high-end appliances. These companies cater to most people with their good, better, and best offerings. While we'll have resources on just about every item one would need, we highlight those products that we stand by.

Again, everything I do is so that the agent can be more productive. With Dakota as a resource we get people through the listing to contract and contract to close phase as efficiently and diligently as possible. The construction business is about engagement and contract to close. Also, it's a resource center for people in the resource trade, whether it's a designer, an architect, an engineer, or a contractor. It's designed to take the consumer through the design and build process more efficiently.

We can have the conversation right there and close on certain parts, many times the most expensive parts, making the other decisions less worrisome. The toughest thing for an agent is to do everything it takes to make the close once the buyer wants renovations done. With Dakota's elegant showroom, in-house talent of designers and contractors, and high end products on hand, my agents can't be beat.

The faster we can get all our clients' questions answered to their satisfaction, the faster we can put it into their budget and the faster the process moves along.

Dakota exudes excellence and caters to those that want the best. We have procured intimate knowledge on high end, high quality products; the type you'd want in a luxury home. To that end, you won't find Chinese cabinets or other products at Dakota that we don't stand behind. We will always refer clients that are looking for that type of quality, but we won't have it represented in our showroom.

Imagine this scenario: three agents discussing with their clients what their needs and wants are for a new kitchen (or a kitchen in their new home). One agent is sitting at a Starbucks, another agent is sitting at the clients' current kitchen, the third agent has the client at their state-of-the-art, stylish showroom actually providing samples for the client to touch and feel, working with a designer on the design of the new kitchen, and showing them the actual products being referred. Which agent provides better service? That's the Ramos way!

Who would you want listing your home? Would you prefer a typical agent or someone who exhibits foresight and is prepared to respond to common objections that will arise during the sale of a particular property? This is part of the reason agents who come to us after being in the business less than three years double their sales. But I'll get more into that a little later.

I have created a service that acts as an in-person Angie's List, if you will. However, instead of looking up all the reviews, setting up appointments, and going through all the running around of picking the right people at the right price, at Dakota, they are all already there. Of course, the client is not forced to use any of our other services, but we believe in the products and services we offer so we recommend them.

As an added support mechanism for my agents, we have a closed Facebook group only privy to my agents and the people — designers, contractors, builders, etc. who are in the collaborative. That way, a question can be answered expertly in a short amount of time. The abundance of cutting edge knowledge in those groups is more than what is taught at most real estate classes.

I can gush on and on about Dakota because it truly is revolutionary for a brokerage, but the best thing to do is to come in and see it for yourself. There's plenty more that sets us apart that I'm excited to share with you.

CHAPTER 6

RAMOS FAMILY OF COMPANIES

Organistics Services

At the heart of it, Organistics is a marketing services and branding company located within our South Tampa office, our first and largest location, although it serves all the agents that would like to take advantage of it. I say it's a branding company and while it's designed to help each individual build their brand, it's also so much more.

Its offerings include social media consulting for optimization and management. If you're an agent and don't have much money to budget for marketing, you can get some traction by leveraging social media. Of course, we also assist with websites, and provide online solutions with a CRM designed for lead generation. Then we help with the "speed to lead" and get those leads converted to a referral.

Every agent knows there's a big difference between a lead and a referral. A lead can be someone that's just kicking tires at a car dealer but may not even have the means to buy the car. A lead isn't worth much. But a referral, that's different. A referral is much more serious about the product or service you offer. A qualified referral is what we all want, someone who wants the product or service, has the means to afford it, and comes from a trusted source. At RE/MAX

Bay to Bay we understand the value of a qualified referral, so Organistics finds leads and, in an efficient manner, identifies them and kicks the referrals to RE/MAX Bay to Bay agents to convert.

We also help the agent get the biggest bang for their buck when it comes to all the different forms of media. There are so many ways to market in print or online that it gets quite confusing and very difficult to generate a positive return on your investment. However, this isn't our first rodeo, so we strive to steer our agents to the outlets that have proven tangible success and greater ROI.

As Adam Contos, the current Chief Operating Officer of RE/MAX LLC said, we are in the people business. So Organistics takes great care to do assessments so that our agents can understand themselves better. This may sound way too "new-age-y" for most brokers but I care about my agents' financial and personal lives. We offer both personal and professional coaching to bring balance to those who feel need it. It's a practice that I hope catches on for the sake of the many agents in this competitive field. We also provide consulting on team building, so that our agents can grow exponentially.

We dedicated 2,000 square feet of space to Organistics. The offices are "white walls" so as meetings are being held, we can write down pertinent information, visible to everyone in the room, and have more productive meetings. As I contemplated about who would be ideal to head up this company, Sheila LaNeve came to my mind because she had a successful coaching practice and is an expert on branding and marketing. I'll let Sheila tell you more about Organistics...

SHEILA LANEVE

"When James approached me about Organistics I was intrigued, however, I had built momentum for the company I owned so I wasn't sure it was right for me. He assured me that I wouldn't have to stop doing what I was doing and asked me to consider it. I have an extensive coaching background and when I heard that part of my responsibilities would be to offer personal life coaching to those who requested it, I was sold on the idea. First and foremost, I love to help others achieve, which is why I decided to partner into Organistics. I haven't looked back since.

"The main goal of Organistics is to provide such a scope of services and support so that RE/MAX Bay to Bay can recruit and retain people who want to be the best. Our focus is on the agent, not just the professional side, but also the personal side."

I don't like to answer needs with just technology, which is why Organistics really works. I know it's unique and different, but that doesn't mean that it's not effective. Many people think they are innovators by investing in a new website; I'm more about the people and processes.

Just a little while ago, we held a major design consultation there for a husband and wife who were seeking to buy a multi-million dollar lot on luxurious Bayshore Boulevard in

Tampa. One of our projectors filled an entire wall and we were able to help them discover exactly what they wanted. Before they left, the husband commented, "I'm so happy we chose the right company to work with."

Those services are perfect for agents to have the credibility to land clients looking for million-dollar homes. That type of client expects more and that's fine with us because we pride ourselves in delivering more.

THE MILLENNIALS ARE HERE

Authors William Straus and Neil Howe are widely credited with coining the term Millennials in 1987. They were referring to children going into preschool in 1982 and who would be graduating high school in the year 2000, ushering us into the new millennium.

You know who they are; you might have one still living in the basement of your house. I'll describe who I'm referring to; the bearded one you only see when he asks for clean clothes and take plates full of food and transforms them into used dishes in the sink. Whether they act like it or not, they're adults... and they're very informed.

Socialmediamarketing.org has this to say about them:

Millennials are known as incredibly sophisticated, technology wise, immune to most traditional marketing and sales pitches... as they not only grew up with it all, they've seen it all and been exposed to it all since early childhood.

To that I'll add that they are much more racially and ethnically diverse, don't like the status quo, don't like 9 to 5 work hours, and don't want to work just to get a paycheck. They want to work someplace that gives their lives more meaning. Also, they hate waiting in line when they can order something online. In terms of real estate, collectively they will soon become the largest home-buying group in the United States. So we have to find a way to cater to this group.

You know what they really like, besides video games? Coffee. They love their coffee, which is one of the reasons I bought a famous coffee brand born in Tampa.

INDIGO COFFEE

If you're in the Tampa Bay area and you haven't tried Indigo Coffee yet, you're missing out on the best coffee in town. Not only do Millennials flock to coffee shops, but a lot of entrepreneurs set up meetings and do a lot of business in coffee shops. Most people who work out of their home would prefer to conduct business in a coffee shop rather than in their home. Our agents are no different. If our three other locations are not convenient, they can meet their clients in downtown Tampa at the Indigo Coffee Shop, owned by Ramos.

It's an elegant, classy café that serves just about every type of coffee/latte people ask for, and it's designed with my agents in mind. Towards the rear, behind glass walls, are mini-offices where my agents take their clients because it's very conducive to conducting business.

I chose Indigo because it was named "Favorite Coffee Spot" in Tampa Bay Business Journals Best in Biz Reader's Choice Awards in 2013. Being that I had managed brands in my previous career, I easily picked up on the strong brand recognition Indigo coffee had in and around Tampa.

Another advantage the coffee shop offers RE/MAX Bay to Bay agents, besides having the absolute coolest place to meet someone in downtown Tampa, is that it is a captive area with high traffic. A captive area is a place such as a hospital, a place where a person is going to stay a while. The average time a person typically spends in a coffee shop is actually longer than going out to eat breakfast. It's typical for business folks, people that are or are going to be homeowners, to spend up to an hour or two in a comfortable coffee shop.

We get to tap into something unseen before in real estate, walk-ins. The Indigo Coffee Shop is on the first floor of a metro area. It gets a ton of traffic. How many walk-ins do you suppose most broker houses get? Near my coffee shop is a Keller-Williams on a second floor. How many walk-ins do you suppose those agents are exposed to? None.

LOCATIONS

We currently have three first class office locations, besides the coffee shop. Our agents can conveniently serve clients in North Tampa, South Tampa, and Palm Harbor, which covers two of the major counties that are considered the Tampa Bay Area. As a third-generation South Tampa native, I've seen the growth and potential of these other two areas and invested in my agents there.

Most agents who work for a brokerage are limited in region because they only have one office. However, people that refer them to their friends or family might live in the area, but not necessarily near their location. I wanted to give my agents a larger playing field. My agents can go to any location to conduct business where they will receive the same level of support.

It's simple really. Being able to intelligently and professionally cater to a larger area gives an agent more opportunity. That's what all the agents really want. That's why the successful ones are great networkers, because they understand that the more people they meet and can talk to, the more opportunities they will have. So now, if an agent in Palm Harbor wants to go to a networking group in North Tampa, they can do so as a "resident" because they have a North Tampa location.

There's a misconception that if there are multiple RE/MAX offices in a city, any RE/MAX agent has access to it, but as I said, it's a misconception. A RE/MAX agent can't just walk into any RE/MAX office and use it. They are independently owned. I share my offices with all my agents. My agents have 24/7 access to all my locations, if they so desire.

If you've been an agent for 15 to 20 years and you've been working the same region for all those years, sure, you have great relationships there and you might be able to maintain a good income, but how will you scale? How can you give yourself a raise if you stay playing in your own backyard?

You have to knock down the fence that holds you in the same three zip codes if you want to make more money in the future. Let's face it, that's what we all want. We don't envision our future selves making the same amount of money year after year. We all want to do better for our families and ourselves. We all want to continue to improve our quality of life and one way to do it is by making more money. It's okay to admit it.

HOW TO SELL MILLION DOLLAR HOMES

Every agent wants to sell million dollar homes. If you meet some that say they don't, don't trust them! They're lying to you.

The problem with tapping into the luxury home market is this — to have high-end clients trust you, you need to have some experience selling luxury homes. Yet, how can you have experience selling high-priced homes if those types of clients don't trust you to sell their homes? That's a conundrum that most agents can't figure out. So, they never get into the luxury homes market, even though that's their ultimate goal.

We've sold million-dollar homes. Actually, we've done more than that, we've actually designed and built million-dollar homes. We, as an organization, have intimate knowledge of those types of structures. A person who invented a widget knows a lot more about that widget than someone who uses it. Apple knows more about the iPhones than the millions of people who use one. IPhone owners in the Tampa area trust the Apple store in Tampa's International

Mall and would travel further to get their iPhone worked on there instead of going to a Sprint or T-Mobile store. Although the retail phone companies sell the same exact phones, they didn't design them, they didn't build them. They'll never know them as well as the people who did. That is the level of knowledge Ramos has in the million-dollar home market.

Our agents can say to a prospective client, with full confidence, "Yes, we have helped buyers and sellers buy and sell million dollar homes, just like yours. In fact, we've built them from the ground up."

The agent may have never sold a million-dollar home, but when you look at the group of more than 100 professionals that I call our team, the agent in fact has sold a million-dollar home because we work together as one. I know coming from a typical brokerage mentality, this may sound Pollyanna, but as the owner and thought leader of our organization, this is fact.

As a team operating as one, we learned how to leverage the playing field to our advantage.

CHAPTER 7

THE POWER OF ONE

With the RE/MAX brand supporting me and my other companies working with synchronicity, I didn't build out your average brokerage. Who wants to be average? The first thing I wanted to do was to ensure that my agents were well respected, not just by their prospects and clients, but by the many industries involved in real estate. Those industries are commonly referred to as vendors.

LEVERAGING VENDORS

Every good agent has tradesmen and other professionals involved in a home buying or selling transaction in his or her contact list. These are the people they refer their clients to in areas that they can't cover, such as plumbing, electrical work, remodeling, etc. Successful and seasoned agents try to use the same people because they have consistently produced good work. The professional level of competence and diligence that these professionals bring to the table make the agent look even better to the client. This is why it is difficult for a new plumber, electrician, home inspection professional, or remodeling company to replace agents' established service providers. It just

67

doesn't happen. In turn, those skilled laborers make sure to continue to do a great job so that the agent continues to use them.

Still, when agents say they have one person that does all their work, it's scary. Sure, he can try to be loyal to the agent, but what if he's working on a big job for the next 60 days when that agent calls?

Even with great go-to people, when the market is on the upswing it's more and more difficult for the agent to keep them because they get to a point where they can cherry pick and work on the best projects for them. An agent could have used a contractor a year ago, but since then that contractor has moved on to higher paying jobs, exclusively working on high-end homes.

The idea of finding a good handyman, a hidden gem, is almost impossible because he's been found already. It gets more and more difficult for an agent to rely on them because the good ones can be more selective about where they work.

It's a full-time job to locate, vet out and get these competent professionals to complete the work. Even the really good agents constantly need to fill their bench with good people because they can't continue to count on the same ones over and over again. The better work they do, the more they can charge, and sooner or later, they'll be too expensive.

THE POWER OF ONE

That's not the case for my agents; we do things a bit differently because our vendors get an incredible amount of business from us. I have found a way to leverage different entities for our agents to secure the best relationships with the best vendors, thus benefitting every agent within the brand. The difference is that with us there is one name that every vendor knows and wants to stay in good terms with — Ramos. Every agent of mine gets the same benefits that I do because they are a part of the Ramos family of companies. They're not viewed as standalone agents who might only bring someone 20 opportunities, they're part of an entity that refers out millions of dollars annually. When someone from our brokerage gives a referral, it's treated with more TLC because the vendors want to ensure that they don't ruin a profitable relationship with me.

It's a win/win for both my agents and our contractors. For the agents, they can refer our contractors with full confidence because:

A. Every vendor on the list has been vetted

B. My approved vendors appreciate the volume we consistently deliver, so they take extra care to accommodate us and make sure they do a great job

C. There's less probability that they will be cherry picked, saving time and money

Even with all the referrals that may come through our network to our vendors, we do realize in a strong market it still may not be enough to maintain true loyalty. I recently acquired a 30,000-square foot warehouse. With it I plan to offer a unique warehousing proposition for the many vendors in the network, specifically smaller hand-to-mouth subcontractors. These subcontractors will have the ability to rent space in 100-square foot increments on a weekly basis. The warehouse will have its own attendant for shipping and receiving, as well as a forklift and various racking capabilities.

You would think what I provide is common for agents who work out of any brokerage, but you'd be wrong. Part of the beauty of being a real estate agent is that you make your own decisions and, in essence, are your own boss. So, if there are ten agents working out of the same brokerage, there could conceivably be ten different electricians being referred to from under the same roof. Now, our agents aren't forced to use the laborers we have established relationships with, but they're happy they have the choice to, because building those relationships is time consuming. Besides, circumstances can change quickly.

As I alluded to earlier, when it comes to verticals in construction and other labor-intensive industries, many issues can arise. For example, an electrician can be on a cruise, a plumber could have been pulled over for a DUI and lost his driver's license (nothing against plumbers, I'm being hypothetical), or someone else could have lost his state license. More common is that their insurance could have lapsed. The agent may have checked his insurance a year ago, but it's no longer valid. An agent doesn't have the time to keep tabs on the many people in his or her contact list. It's embarrassing for an agent to refer someone who no longer works in that field or has a terrible reputation.

My agents can spend their valuable time networking, marketing themselves, and finding great opportunities — doing what they're really good at. It makes the office much more efficient and, more importantly, delivers better value for the client as the agent is viewed as professional and well prepared.

I set my brokerage up like this because before I entered the market, when I was in the process of my 18 moves — buying, selling, and building homes — the agents I utilized were quick to give me the numbers of roofers, plumbers, etc. At first I was pleased that I didn't have to find the people I needed, but after going through that scenario many times, I surmised that the agents were thinking more about hurrying me to close so they could collect their 3 percent commission than actually trying to help me. I say that because at times the people I was referred to appeared less than trustworthy. Some were no longer licensed, while others no longer did what I was told they did. Every agent meant well, they really did, they just didn't end up having the resources they told me they had because things change so fast. Once I took on the rigors of vetting the right contractors, handymen, and other skilled tradesmen, I realized it wasn't the agent's fault. It was like having another full-time job.

As part of the Ramos family, my agents don't have to worry

about any of that.

HARNESS THE MILLIONS

In any given job that requires some form of demolition, whether it's from the ground up or a renovation, up to 30 different verticals could be involved. In most cases, a good agent has obtained a certain level of influence over the homeowners and guides them on who to hire for each particular job. An agent who sells 30 homes a year potentially refers more than $1 million worth of references!

A good agent is valuable to a good vendor. Now consider this: if an entire brokerage vets a company and that company gets the bulk of the referrals from its many agents, how valuable do you think that relationship would be for the vendor?

Those that sign up for my program as a third-party vendor undergo a triage-type process where we match the request with the best service vendor for the job based on size, manpower, and experience. By matching the right vendors to the jobs best suited for them we continuously get great results. Our vendors realize the importance of our relationship. We've referred more than $100 million worth of business since we opened our doors. In the next 12 months, we project to refer out at least $50 million. And because we are growing exponentially, it is logical to assume that the trend will continue.

We have worked hard and smart to establish relationships with the best manufacturer reps and the best talent in the Tampa Bay area. However, some of the business, depending on the vertical, we no longer refer out. We refer in. And that's what sets up Ramos to lead the way into the future.

As I didn't set out to build an average brokerage, I didn't want to be a typical leader. I didn't want just anyone to come in and work for me, I wanted the best people to come in so I could work for them.

CHAPTER 8

SERVANT LEADERSHIP

There's a twisted misconception of many people in charge of being "The Boss." It's been wrong for centuries. Many years ago, people that had positions of power and influence used it to make their subordinates subservient to them. Not much has changed.

The common misconception many leaders have is that those they are leading are there to serve him or her. This is known as the bureaucratic leadership style. It's the same sort of leadership that rulers deployed in the days of ancient Egypt when they forced slaves to build pyramids and worship them as gods. While the whole "worship me, I'm a God" thing doesn't work today, many managers, owners, and leaders still subscribe to the "It's my way or the highway" philosophy. People in managerial roles still try to use people for their own personal and professional gains. There are so many egotistical "leaders" out there that I would go as far to say that everyone has been subjected to a bad manager/supervisor/boss at one time or another. Thankfully, I don't subscribe to that style of leadership.

I'm privileged to have more than 100 full-time professionals work at the Ramos companies. Some are my employees and many are independent contractors, but regardless of the type of relationship we have, they all look to me for leadership. I value that. In fact, I appreciate their talent and time so much that my philosophy is not that they work for me, but it is I that work for them. That's called Servant Leadership.

As I've gained experience and worked for incredibly bright mentors, I've learned that your title doesn't define you, nor does the amount of people you employ. The profit and loss sheet doesn't define you either. Who you are is what defines you!

Many people foresee themselves being better versions of themselves if they make more money or get a bigger title. They see themselves as perhaps more philanthropic, more patient, and calmer individuals. But let me tell you this — if you don't change who you are now, a position with more responsibility or authority will not suddenly recreate you.

Abraham Lincoln once said: "Nearly all men can stand adversity, but if you want to test a man's character, give him power."

Many people misconstrue the meaning of management by labeling it leadership. They would be incorrect. You can be a manager and not be a leader. I've known business owners that weren't even the leaders of their own companies. When a manager talks, people listen. When a leader talks, people listen and then do what the leader said to do. It is very uncommon to find a natural born leader in the business world. Sure, there are some men in the armed forces that have lead their unit(s) to overcome seemingly insurmountable odds and they've been labeled as born leaders. However, those generals all went to Officer's Candidate School (OCS).

Leadership is a skill. It can be taught, practiced, and perfected. One can learn how to be a better influencer and a more sincere listener and still be assertive and hold people accountable.

When I worked at General Mills, Unilever, and PepsiCo, I shot up through the ranks. I felt the sky was the limit for me. However, I got to a certain point that they wouldn't let me pass. The high-level executive positions were taken and when they became available, it was as if their replacements were already grandfathered in. Yet I continued to surpass the expectations placed on me and was deserving of more. But there was nowhere else for me to go.

Have you ever seen an organizational chart? They look like pyramids, with the CEO as the sole person at the top. There's always only one. The time comes when overachievers reach a point where the company cannot promote them anymore. There's not enough room in the org chart for another person. That's when many companies get creative. They tell them it's time for the overachiever to broaden his or her experiences.

That's what happened to me. I couldn't get promoted, but the companies wanted to keep me. So when I reached a certain point, they told me I needed a challenge, perhaps knowing how much I loved challenges. They wanted to give me recognition and keep me motivated so I wouldn't leave them. So they tried to disguise a quasi promotion in the form of doing the same thing somewhere else.

For me it went something like this: "Great job, James, I can't tell you how happy we are with you. You've exceeded our expectations with what you did with Publix. Now, to get you more experience, we want you to move to San Francisco and call on Safeway, Inc."

Naturally, I was happy that they had seen my work and valued me. However, as the conversation continued, I realized that they were giving me a lateral move, not a promotion. They wanted me to go to San Francisco to call on Safeway, Inc. and if that went well, they wanted to relocate me to Arkansas to call on Wal-Mart. Basically, I was looking at another decade of lateral moves and relocations before even having a conversation regarding a promotion. Moving your family to a city where you don't know anyone isn't easy. We had done it multiple times but it was no longer okay for me to go where they sent me, and as soon as they couldn't squeeze any more juice from me in that area, dip me into another city to squeeze me all over again. It seemed that for all the success I did for them, I was paid with lateral moves.

I've been a part of a myriad of re-orgs and different hierarchal shuffling, only to find myself in the same position. I learned a lot in corporate America, including what not to do.

The traditional organizational chart mindset is not limited to just large companies, the smallest of companies operate the same way. That's pretty much the way most businesses are run. But in case you haven't realized it, I like to push the envelope. I don't like to do what everyone else does for the sole reason because that's how it's been done for years. I look at how I believe things ought to be done. I clear it with my conscience and check to see if it aligns with my ethics and then run it through to see if it mirrors my core values. When I started in real estate, I designed a different organization chart. It currently looks like this:

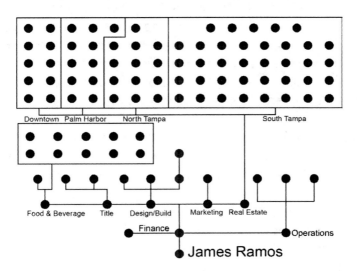

You might notice that my organizational chart is a reverse pyramid. I'm at the bottom! I work for my managers and our collective staff. It's up to me to find a way to be useful to them so that they can reach their professional potential.

Zig Ziglar said it best; *"You can have anything you want*

in life if you just help enough other people get what they want."

I have a big vision, big dreams. It's made up of many goals; some are at arm's reach and others are loftier, harder to reach. However, I know that I'll never reach my goals by myself. I need help from talented professionals and the best way to get them to help me is to help them.

I'm out to build the absolute best brokerage in the world, starting with the Tampa Bay area. I can't do that with people that want to eke out a living. I want to align myself with people that want to be the best. Those are the type of people that won't settle for anything less than working for the best brokerage in the world. So, to that end, I look for people who are serious about being successful and ask them how I can be of best service to them.

I need to understand what my staff wants to do and what makes them tick. I want to know what motivates them to get out of bed in the morning. And, within reason, I try to eliminate tasks they're not so good at to allow them to focus on those things they're really good at, allowing them a better opportunity to excel.

I sought assistance as I prepared to write this book. I wanted to give you a real look at the culture in my office, so key members of my team were interviewed. Here is a look at Ramos through their eyes.

Galyn Lecher — General Manager, Suncoast Title
If colors were named as qualities, one would find James has a myriad of them. He is a loyal man of truth, integrity, compassion, inspiration, and positivity, while always remaining humble in his servant style of leadership.

He is also an unstoppable driving force who will do whatever it takes to finish the task, overcome the obstacle, and meet the goal set before him. He is armed with intelligence, talent, and resources, which he uses with military precision. Spend but a few moments with him and you will find that he emanates all the characteristics of what one looks for in a leader.

Kevin Walsh — CFO
In his heart, James likes to create. The culture he has fostered, with different entities, communicate effectively with each another, allowing everyone to do their jobs at a high level.

I would be remiss if I didn't mention his high level of energy and the positive vibe he exudes. He doesn't sit back; he's always moving forward.

Tony Garcia — VP of Operations, Ramos Design Build
When people find out I drive from Georgia to Florida every week to go to work, they often ask me why I do it. If I had to condense all the reasons down to one, it would be because of James Ramos. He is a man with great vision, and the fact that he not only talks about it, but acts on it, is exhilarating.

The difference between him and other builders is that he personally takes an interest in the jobs; he doesn't just hand them over. Also, the fact that he's aligned us with fantastic companies like The Galley, Bremtown Cabinets, and Fox Blocks is brilliant. If I were an agent, I would not be anywhere other than RE/MAX Bay to Bay for the simple fact that no other broker provides as many services. A leader doesn't just talk, a leader leads. That's James.

Judy Eaves — RE/MAX Bay to Bay
The biggest reason why I wanted to work with James Ramos is because of James Ramos. I love how he thinks out of the box, his class, and his entrepreneurial mindset. He's a visionary who isn't afraid to take action.

Jill Lifsey — District Designs, Dakota Kitchen & Bath
I've had a positive experience working with James. He's very creative and forward-thinking. He has used technology in a way that embodies servant leadership. For example, in any transaction that's conducted through the brokerage, and there are many, I'm one click away from being added, as a service provider, by way of our transaction software. This avoids the typical referral by way of management. If you're an agent who needs a designer, you don't even have to call me, you can make the introduction to your client by one click on your smartphone. James trusts people to do their job and empowers them with decision-making capabilities, and that's refreshing.

Robert Pynn — Superintendent, Ramos Design Build
After serving in the United States Marine Corps during the Reagan Administration, I got into construction. I was

always fascinated with it. After many years in the industry, a mutual acquaintance told me about what James was doing. He described James as a visionary and said his company had legs.

I saw his number on a sign and gave him a call. He called me back the following week and after a great conversation, he put me on. He liked what I brought to the table and added me on as a full-time employee and I catapulted to the superintendent role. My friend was 100 percent correct; James is a visionary, but he's also much more. He's loyal, honest, and fair to work for. We have done amazing projects together and under his leadership I know many more are coming.

David Bolton — Realtor® at RE/MAX Bay to Bay

I love James' fresh concept towards real estate. He goes far beyond the typical buy and sell, also getting into the design, build, and furnish aspects, which is great because anytime I can add value to my clients, it sets me apart.

James has the perfect balance of hands on, hands off. When he hires thoroughbreds, he doesn't hold them back. He's very protective of his brand, which is great for me because I don't want to associate my name with a brand that doesn't care about their reputation.

Sheila LaNeve — VP of Marketing, Organistics

I've known James for years; our sons went to the same school. One day, before my son's birthday party, I faced one of the most difficult times of my life. During the party I was still a wreck and told a few of the parents my situation.

I didn't know what to do, but James helped me.

He showed me other homes that would be more conducive to my situation, which was hard for me to do on my own. He was very helpful throughout the ordeal, at times checking in on me, asking "Do you need help in moving?" or "How's everything going?" Coincidentally, my dad had passed and his name was James. In a way, I felt that my dad was still connected with me through James Ramos.

This was long before I ever worked with him. It spoke volumes of his compassion and values as a person and he exhibits the same characteristics in the office.

James has taken a lot of time to recognize his strengths and weaknesses. He's highly aware of what he's good at and focuses his time there. He spends time weekly improving himself with what's important to him. He encourages others to do the same. For James, family is at the top. He's very loyal and extends trust to those that work with him."

He is aware of his core values and consistently lives a life aligned with his values. I believe that when someone lives like that, life works.

But one of the best things about working with him is that he's not afraid to admit making a mistake. I've seen people approach him who were unhappy and instead of him defending the way things are, I've seen him say, "Let's fix it," thus encouraging open communication.

In case you're reading the term servant leadership for the first time, I didn't invent it. It's been around for a long, long time. I had always exhibited characteristics of a servant leader but it wasn't until I read the book called "The Servant," by James C. Hunter, that I fully adopted the philosophy. I highly recommend you read "The Servant." It shifted my mindset. Here are some of my favorite quotes from it:

Authority is always built on service and sacrifice.

Leadership is not about personality, possessions, or charisma, but all about who you are as a person.

I used to believe that leadership was about style, but now I know that leadership is about substance, namely character.

To have a healthy and thriving business, there must be healthy relationships with the CEOS. in the organization and I'm not referring to the Chief Executive Officers. I am talking about the Customers, the Employees, the Owner (or stockholders), and the Suppliers.

As Sheila said, I'm aware of my strengths and weaknesses and I know what I'm good at. I try to keep my focus there and believe that the rest will follow. I trust the people that share my vision, but at times things aren't always hunky dory.

At times a servant leader can become so immersed in introspection and encouraging employees to look inward for meaning that the company's bottom line can suffer. Also, when a leader is so dedicated to serving his employees, it can make him a target for manipulators, which is why one must be guided by their morals and ethics and align it with their goals.

As a servant leader, I address the responsibilities of everyone on staff. We attempt to be very transparent. For example, I have monthly financial meetings where we discuss what to keep doing, what we need to stop doing, and what we need to start doing. Everyone knows his or her assigned roles.

The way I lead is not something I just flip a switch and turn on. People who try to be what they're not are always exposed. I try my best to live according to the ethics and standards I've set for myself.

I fully undertake the responsibility that's upon me. As I mentioned earlier, I grew up with my dad being a general contractor and I graduated with a degree in Economics. I realize the different subject matters I need to be an expert in. I have taken the time to study the landscape I compete in, and to know intimately the best processes of getting all our jobs done. I've also taken great care to learn how to express my ideas in a manner that will inspire, motivate, and make people want to work together.

I'm also smart enough to know that I'm not that smart in many areas. So I look for people smarter than me and give them all the support I can. It makes no sense to hire a great guitarist to play bass just because he also plays bass. If I need a bass player, I'm going to hire a great bass player. In my businesses and business relationships, I work with top quality people. While it's my name on the marquee sign, in my office I often have people telling me what needs to be done for them to be most effective. We brainstorm, collaborate, agree on a plan, and execute at a high level.

When you work with so many people who are striving to excel, it helps you raise your game. It's like deciding whether to golf with your buddies who just want to drink, or with Tiger Woods. If you golf with your drinking buddies, you laugh at the worst shots and are more worried that you're going to run out of beer before you finish, instead of your technique and score. That's similar to working in a brokerage with part-timers and people who are looking to just get by. Those aren't my type of people. Now, if you golf with Tiger, you're going to soak in every bit of advice he gives you and put all of your attention and energy into every shot. After a short time, your golf game will improve dramatically. It's the same with Ramos. By working with smart people who are driven to succeed, you will improve at the tasks you need to perform.

As I write this, I believe that it might come across as self-serving on my part. After all, I'm writing about how well I lead. But although it's uncomfortable for me to toot my own horn this way, I think it's important for you to know who I am. If you're a real estate agent or thinking of becoming one, I want you to seriously consider Ramos as a place to call home.

I guess the best way to prove my leadership style is with

the facts. Here's some of my "proof in the pudding." I started my brokerage in 2011 and since then we've won multiple awards, have four locations, a coffee shop, and over a hundred professionals working together. If I wasn't the type of servant leader I say I am, I doubt I could have attracted that many savvy professionals, nor grown at the rate we've experienced. Most of the people associated with Ramos have doubled their previous income. Some people and vendors in my circle have made four times their previous salary! I'm incredibly proud of that. Not just proud of myself, because there's no way I could've done this by myself. I'm proud of the people working with me and the culture we have all bought into.

Investing in people is the single most important part of my job. I find that to be the most important thing a leader must do. That, my friends, is what being a servant leader is. That's what I strive to be day in and day out.

CHAPTER 9

TEAM BUILDING

Sometimes great leaders are defined by building great teams. John Wooden, an American college basketball coach who won a record 10 national championships over a 12-year span at UCLA, is known as arguably the most successful coach of any professional sport. The many awards and accolades he received include being inducted to the Basketball Hall of Fame in 1973, receiving the Reagan Distinguished American Award in 1995, and also receiving the Presidential Medal of Freedom in 2003.

He brought a new attitude to the UCLA Bruins basketball team, a program that had never achieved much success. He is known for instilling much-needed discipline to his teams, including forbidding them to curse or criticize each other. He also repeated these phrases over and over again: *"Never Lie, Never Cheat, Never Steal"* and *"Earn The Right To Be Proud And Confident."* If you played on his team, you most likely heard these sayings too: *"Never Score Without Acknowledging A Teammate"*, *"One Word Of Profanity And You're Done For The Day,"* and *"Treat Your Opponent With Respect."*

He also was not afraid to treat everyone equally, including

his best players. One of my favorite stories about his leadership style took place after UCLA won a national championship with Bill Walton, who had just won the National Player of the Year award, playing center. Bill was known for his affinity for the "hippie" lifestyle. After traveling the country, touring with "The Grateful Dead," and "finding himself," Bill came to basketball camp with a full-grown beard and long hair; something John Wooden had said was not permissible.

Practice was set to start in about 15 minutes when John saw Bill. Bill was ready for the speech. He told his coach that it was his right as a citizen of the United States of America to keep a beard and long hair if he wanted to. It was also a form of self-expression against the status quo that many in his generation found unfair. He told his coach that, although he respected him, he had no right to tell him how to grow his hair. In fact, Bill said he gave John the best speech he had ever given in his life.

When he was done, John complimented Bill for coming to terms with who he was as a person, also for growing such a nice beard. Then he said, and I'm paraphrasing here,

"Thank you for all your hard work and dedication to the team. We sure will miss you."

Bill said, "But it's my right to wear my hair how I want to."

John said, "You're right Bill, it's your right. But it's my right to determine who plays on this team."

Bill fumed for a moment until John looked at his watch and said, "You have 14 minutes."

Bill ran down the hall and out the door, jumped on his bike and pedaled to the nearest barber and asked him to just take most of his hair off. He then got a cheap razor and went back to the facility where he shaved outside the gym with cold water. Bill snuck into practice five minutes late, hoping his coach wouldn't notice. John didn't notice, or at least he didn't show Bill that he had. They went on to win another championship and a freshly shaved, clean cut Bill Walton heaved his coach on his shoulders and paraded him among thousands of cheering fans.

Great leaders build great teams. In the previous chapter I shared with you my leadership style. Now I want to get into how we support our agents with building a team and the team that makes this happen. In other words, it takes a team to support our agents who want to build a team.

TEAM BUILDING

The question some agents have is, "why build a team?" Their rationale is that they went into real estate to be their own boss, to work independently. That was part of what lured them into the industry. That's probably why so many agents work for themselves. I get it. I mean, I don't understand why you would want to do every little thing but if you want to be independent. That's fine.

That doesn't work for me or the agents I attract. My goals exceed my capabilities, so I need a strong team around me.

The agents that work in my organization also have their sights set on achieving goals that would be impossible to accomplish on their own.

I had to build a team because my vision required it. I'm an ambitious person and I'm not ashamed of it in the slightest. My vision was birthed through my ambition. I don't want to be just another brokerage owner. I don't want to give the same support as everyone else, and I don't want for my agents to be run-of-the-mill agents. So for us, being a part of a well working team is perfect. The team that I'm referring to is the entire organization inclusive of all the staff and agents, even those who have their own agent team. We are one, one team.

TEAM

The word "team" can mean different things: a number of persons forming one of the sides of a game or contest, or two or more harnessed animals (horse or oxen) pulling the same wagon or plow. It can even mean a family of young animals, like ducks or pigs. But in business, of course, it means something different. The word team brings with it an implication of synergy and working together for a common goal. In real estate, a team can be two people such as a husband and wife, good friends or associates that appreciate the other's work ethic or popularity — or it can be a mega team. Teams can be easy to form but much harder to keep together over years.

I recently attended an educational summit where Brian Buffini, one of the top real estate coaches in the country, was teaching. He had spent a large portion of his real estate career in developing, in his own words, "effective, productive, and happy teams." What he focused on were agent teams. Not the team it takes to support the agent. But in any case, there I was, in a crowd of agents who had paid good money to learn how to best grow their businesses and Buffini did not disappoint.

He said, "The number one reason to build an agent team is to best manage an influx of leads."

I thought long and hard on that, and on more of what he said, and began to think of the perfect team that my agents needed. Agents have to do so much by themselves. They market themselves, go to networking groups, manage their online presence (social media, website, blogs), make the initial calls, gather information, and so on and so forth just to get a listing. An agent who works by him or herself is severely outgunned in the marketplace. Earlier I wrote that just keeping tabs on the vendors and having a bench of people to assist from contract to close was like another full-time job. Add to that everything I wrote here that they need to do to get a listing and it's nearly impossible for just one person to be ultra successful. Even something simple, such as sending out letters, isn't as easy as it sounds. The agent needs to write the letter, make the copies, put each one in an envelope, write the address down on a sticky, stamp it, and then go somewhere to mail it.

But many agents feel that hiring someone full-time is irresponsible on their part because at times it takes too long for them to get paid and to hire someone hourly doesn't work for them. So you have agents who are amazing in front of a prospect but spend very little time in front of prospects because they are doing every other little thing it takes to stay on the forefront of people's minds and manage the business. The Ramos way is a much better way. We set out to build a team that answers the needs of the agent and helps them in their selling process. First, we needed to understand the logical steps that we consider value-added if it was done for them.

There are five major areas of concern for an agent — the lead, qualifying the lead, the conversion, the preparation to get to the contract stage, and the contract to close stage. Here's a quick snapshot of what the team I've assembled in-house does.

1) Get the Lead
A qualified lead is the bloodline of real estate. Much of what an agent does is centered on it. We have the ability to generate leads from a multitude of sources, and many leads at that.

2) Qualify the Lead
We contact the prospect five minutes after we get the lead and gather vital information so that the agent is prepared for the call. If the lead is worthy, it becomes a referral.

3) Convert the Referral
If it's a buyer, find them a home. If it's a seller, get the listing. (This is the role of the agent.)

4) Get the contract
We support our agents with all the market analysis to help

them get to the contract stage.

5) Contract to Close Management
We manage this convoluted area and its many moving parts.

Here's a more detailed explanation:

We have a service called Organistics Services that will take care of an agent's online activities. In this marketing company we manage their social media and their website, and even do some blogging. We also handle their SEO, banners, Google Adwords, and do everything else to keep the agent visible online. They approve of everything and remain autonomous. When a lead comes in from our efforts, we call the interested party in fewer than five minutes. Then we act as a triage and ask 15 important questions to assess what stage the person is in. We then give the lead, fully developed, to the agent thus converting the lead into a referral.

Many agents who handle this on their own know what it's like when a lead comes in. If they're driving when it comes in they pull to the side of the road and hurry to contact the lead, hoping a lot of time hadn't elapsed already, and start a sometimes-awkward conversation because they don't have any tangible data on them. During this conversation they attempt to write down notes on paper, which eventually end up being typed into their phone or computer, making them duplicate the process.

Our agents who utilize this service get the lead with so much information it is now called a referral. They know if the person wants to buy or sell in 15 days or in 90, thus they'll know how to prioritize their immediate time. They also know vital bits of information before they even talk to them, such as when's the best time to call, their price range, the locations they desire, and most importantly if they are pre-qualified. If they're not pre-qualified, we're ready to refer it to a mortgage banker. The best part here is for the potential customer. He or she has been contacted promptly and has begun the process of working with the brokerage before the agent has even called.

For some, we offer a deeper level of service, where my team creates a competitive marketing analysis so the agent can get a listing presentation fully prepared. They can have an agreement in their briefcase that's ready to go, complete with prospects' names typed in and a recommended price of the home in question sourced from one of our analysts. If the client decides to sign on with the agent, the agent can present the document for a wet signature or they can hand over an iPad and the client can write their signature with a finger. Whether the client signs by pen or through the iPad, it goes to a coordinator who initiates the next steps, be it contacting a photographer, preparing marketing material, or setting up the listing in the multiple listing service.

Once it gets to the contract stage, we offer a contract to close coordinator. Oftentimes there's due diligence on the buyer side that needs to be done. We handle all of that. And lastly, currently in a test phase, if you're an agent, you hate waiting for the appraisers and other service professionals because they give you a timeframe like cable guys who tell you they'll be there between 1 p.m. and 5 p.m. We actually have someone waiting there at the location!

If an agent is a home run hitter, this gives him or her the liberty to swing away and knock as many face-to-face interactions with their clients as they can out of the park while all of the other details are being professionally tended to.

The benefits of being part of such a team are many, but I'll touch upon just two:

1. It's much more cost-efficient to work with the Ramos team for all these things than to hire a full-time employee who you not only pay a salary to, but also the benefits and at times their travel mileage, etc.

2. If you hire an employee, you have to train him or her. It takes a long time for someone to learn how to expertly handle every little transaction, including dealing with vendors, upholding the ethics, and always representing you the way you would like. At Ramos, this is all some people do, and they're experts at it. They've been through the construction, renovation, design, and furnish phase. You won't find an employee with this type of training.

If you're an agent, you don't deserve anything less than this level of support. This is the new way of being successful in real estate. The future of brokerages is right here in the Tampa Bay area. We pride ourselves in supporting our agents and allowing them to do the things they love to do because they're good at it. Go to your networking lunches, go to the after-work gathering, or go treat a potential client to a round of golf. We will ensure that everything else is handled while you do what you're good at.

When an agent comes to Ramos, they can bring their team, build a team, or they can use the team already assembled here. It's their choice. All I want to do is to offer the right types of services for those who want to take advantage of them.

Teams that win championships know their roles and execute them to perfection. I've built the infrastructure of a championship team. However, each team needs a leader. That just might be you.

GENERATIONAL WEALTH

I would say that 90 percent of people would like to be independently wealthy. To make enough money that their generations — their children, grandchildren, and great grandchildren — can lean on to do great things for themselves and others. I would also say that the other 10 percent are lying. I can't imagine that anyone wouldn't want to leave behind such a legacy.

The problem is, how to do it? How do you create the type of wealth that will allow you to retire earlier than you expected and build a better foundation for your children that was left for you? I'm no motivational speaker and I'm not an eternal optimist, the facts are that most people will not achieve that type of financial status in their lifetime. However, the facts are also that some people will. But it would be impossible to do so without following some sort of plan. While there are different ways to accrue wealth, I can only speak of one by experience. It's not that I'm mega wealthy, but I have a plan to get there and I'm going to share it with you.

A person's salary (including commission checks) will most

likely not make you enough money to pass on to future generations. The way I see it, the best way to accrue real wealth is to add passive income to whatever you're making now. I'm not referring to getting a part-time job at Target or to be a hired clown on weekend birthday parties for kids. What I mean, and this is really for real estate agents, is to leverage the knowledge and expertise you've already accrued and use it for your own personal gain.

Listen to me well real estate agent, and I say this with respect and admiration: 3 percent commissions are not going to give you generational wealth. Sadly, most of you have no idea, or don't have the perception that you actually work in a diamond mine. You've found countless homes for your clients, most of the time for less money than they are worth. Or you've helped them build out or renovate a room to make it even more valuable. Hey, that's the job, right? You find these gems (homes) and deliver them to the clients. You get a testimonial or two on how you've helped your client make an extra $15,000 in one transaction and that's great. But... why haven't you considered doing the same thing for yourself?

You're working for a percentage and you might be making a decent living at it. However, working for a percentage is vastly different than working for equity. And that's where the money is.

You are intimately involved in the buying and selling of homes. You know contractors, painters, roofers, and maybe even people that work for the city, and you leverage them for other people's big gains so you can get a small percentage. Are you starting to see the flaw in that way of thinking when it relates to building generational wealth?

I want to encourage you to maximize the license you've earned. Find that one diamond in the rough, the one that you know in your heart can be a fantastic investment, and keep it for yourself. There's nothing wrong with it. It's not unethical. You've been around the real estate block a few times and you know the outcome, you know that the story will end with you making potentially tens of thousands of dollars in one shot if you flip a house, or that it will bring in money monthly if you decide to rent it.

The problem most people encounter is that they say they don't have the money. I'm speaking from experience. I used to have that mindset too. I'll never forget the story I'm about to share with you because it shifted my mindset and marked my life. I was visiting my friend and mentor, Fran Williams, in Niagara Falls, New York and we were talking about life; you know, family, sports, career, and everything else you talk to a trusted friend about. When we got to the point of how I was doing in my various businesses, I sort of hung my head and confided to him...

"My biggest challenge is that I'm being held back."

"How are you being held back?" he asked.

"I come across all sorts of opportunities that I would love to capitalize on, but I don't have the money nor the means to take advantage of all the opportunities that come my way," I lamented.

I could never have expected his reaction. He had a field day with what I said. He went on for a good 30 minutes on how much my statement upset him. I can't tell you everything he said, but he did call me out. He was flabbergasted to know how much money I had made others, whether it be on the find or the build of a residence. He also reminded me of the many shareholders I generated profits for when I was in corporate America. It was like I was throwing a little pity party for myself in his home, because I did not have the means to take advantage of my opportunities. He had no time for that kind of talk.

"James, you are in the eye of the storm. You know real estate. You know what would be a great investment and what won't. Why are you worried about money?"

Then he said this and it changed my life: "Find the opportunity, the money will come."

I realized that I had been focusing on the wrong thing. I was operating from a mindset of scarcity and not of abundance. It was a pivotal moment in my life. It was as if a weight was lifted off my shoulders. He forced me to look in the mirror and to stop making excuses for myself.

"It's time to follow your passion, James. You're in the perfect position to do so."

I left New York a changed man. I hope that when you read this, it also changes your mindset. I saw opportunity that I had to invest money in, and others I had to invest time in. Today, my development business is credited with more than 100,000 square feet of new luxury construction in the Tampa Bay area and has provided a phenomenal return for our investors.

Have you ever heard an athlete described as "a student of the game?" It's a compliment, referring to how smart the player is. But it's a disguise in that it really means that the organization has hopes for the player to potentially be a part of their organization well past his playing days, perhaps as a coach or manager. My advice for you is to keep doing what you need to do to be successful today, but also become a student of the game. Our game is real estate.

You've accrued such a great number of skills. Identify the areas where you're not so good at and study them. You already have skill sets in your bag, spend 5 percent cultivating where you're not as versed and become a complete player. Tell people who trust you and who have the means to invest that you've identified a property where they can make an immediate 15 percent, and then another 15 percent a year, the money will come! Trust me.

Once you buy an investment property, you have a choice to make — fix it and flip it, or rent it. Many people go for the quick cash and that's okay. They do so because it will only take 6-12 months of their lives instead of being a long-term process. Most people don't want to go through the process of becoming property managers. After all, it's not the easiest of things to do. You have to ensure that the space is livable, market it, find someone to pay the rent who's going to pay on time and leave it in as good shape as they found it. And throughout the years you have to be the point of contact for the many calls/complaints whenever they have an issue.

But here's the thing, owning the property — being the landlord — does not mean you have to also be the property manager. You can make passive income while someone else handles the day-to-day activities. Because I'm in the property management business, I can attest to its merits for the landlords. If you would rather not manage the property, you can lean on the resources of your brokerage. Today my brokerage manages hundreds of properties in the Tampa Bay area. I'm proud to say we have a handful of the best property managers in our great city. Yet, most brokers don't want to bear the responsibilities of managing property, but as you've read, I'm not like most brokers.

If you have aspirations to retire at some point and to create the sort of passive income that you can gift to your offspring, it behooves you to study the real estate market that you specialize in and jump right into it. Here's a tip: once you find the right opportunity, don't wait.

REAL ESTATE DEVELOPMENT

When you think of a real estate developer, Donald Trump might come to mind. I don't want to focus on The Donald as this is not the place for political ramblings. But my point is that many people believe they need to already have tremendous wealth to become a real estate developer. Well, I would beg to differ. Real estate developers come in all shapes and sizes. And you don't have to deal in hotels to generate impressive returns on your investment. I know a thing or two about real estate development because it's the center of what I do.

I don't have Trump-money and I don't have experience in building entire neighborhoods or 50 story high-rises, but I'm still a real estate developer. I love to innovate and create beautiful homes. I specialize in building million-dollar homes because I love the challenge involved in it. The clients I cater to as a developer are the hardest to please. They expect nothing less than excellence and excellence isn't easy to obtain. Therein lies the challenge. Most developers would like to play in this space, thinking it's luxury homes so it must mean big bucks, but they don't realize the temperaments of the consumers who can afford million dollar homes.

The challenge is exhilarating. It's as close to the competition I basked in when I played Division 1 baseball. Standing at the plate, bat in hand, with the student body watching, as a pitcher that can throw a heater at 90 miles per hour is winding up... I love situations like that! The find, the design, and development, and ultimate sale of these high-end deals is just as intense. It's like a game of high-stakes poker. To do the fulfillment part, to design and build and furnish a breathtaking home that the client absolutely loves... that's a rush! It brings out the best in me.

You can become a real estate developer the same way you eat an elephant, one bite at a time. Look around at your network, your team. Not just those you might employ, but everyone around you who helps your business run smoothly. If you're an agent in my organization just look at the team your brokerage has put together. Then, find a home that needs some TLC that you can get a good CAP rate. Get a 10-13 percent return on your investment and do it again, and again, and then two at a time, and then more. Where else can you invest in something tangible that also brings joy to others? Out of all the people you know in your life, you're the one with the inside track on everything real estate. Maximize your position.

INVESTMENT FUND

My family has been in construction in and around the Tampa Bay area since 1956, as I mentioned before. My four brothers are also in the construction business in one form or another. I have signs all over the city with my name on it in big, bold letters. Suffice to say, I get a lot of calls, sometimes from people mistaking me for one of my brothers, but still, I get a lot of calls from people with real estate needs. One call particularly helped me grow exponentially.

A man called me because his father had passed away and left them a nice property. His two siblings and he agreed to sell it and voted him as the one to handle the estate. He had met with two agents prior to calling me and told me that the property was a double lot and was worth $650,000, but was interested in selling it as soon as possible for $550,000.

"How much time can you give me to look into it?" I asked.

"My plan is to call a few other builders, but I'll give you till tomorrow."

I immediately stopped what I was doing and went to work on it. Like a pilot, I first checked the instruments in front of me. I checked out the property online, verified the value of the home in the Hillsborough county tax records, scoped out the neighborhood etc. After everything checked out okay, I went to see it in person. On my way there I called the city official I know who's in construction services and inquired if the property is a candidate for a split lot. He told me it was, but that also, due to the commercial property surrounding it, it was also a candidate to become a commercial property. That was great news!

At that point, I had not built an investment network; all I had to rely on for investments was my wife, Connie, and myself. My construction line was on another project and I needed 45 days for the financing to come through. I called him back and made him the offer.

"Thanks for getting back to me so quickly, James, but we have a cash offer on the table. The buyer is going to close on Friday."

I was bummed out. I lost out on the deal and, as competitive as I am, I don't like to lose. But instead of walking away with hurt feelings, I looked internally at my process to see why I lost out on that opportunity. I realized that I didn't have extra funds for situations like that. Out of all the friends I have and people in the business who look to me for sound advice and leadership, I had not leveraged them into an investment network where we could all benefit. I thought about all the people who call me for real estate advice before they buy a property and came up with a big list of wealthy and influential people. I swore to never be outgunned like that again. So I sought out the assistance of my CFO, Kevin Walsh, and our knowledgeable legal team and 90 days later the Ramos Investment Fund was created.

Now, if you think I take building beautiful luxury homes seriously, it pales in comparison with the responsibility I feel managing a family's wealth through our investments. I created a package that people can't refuse. They understand my expertise in finding a great opportunity to invest in, evaluate it, acquire it at a price that fits our needs, design it, execute the construction plan, see it through to a certificate of occupancy, warranty the property, list it, market it, and sell it so that everyone who invested in it comes out a winner. I have created an investment package that people don't say no to, in fact, they thank me for including them.

You can do the same if you are so inclined. You have much of the same knowledge I do. I'm not a rocket scientist; I just know how to leverage the tools at my disposal to add additional revenue streams into my personal bank account. I ask my agents to take a good hard look at the hurdles they put before them. They'll find that some lack real substance, and for the rest, all you need is the faith to step out and develop the pieces you don't currently have.

When we get a client, all they want us to do is to create equity for them. That's the bare bones of it. When they ask, "What do you think?" They're really asking if they will come out winning. If the answer is yes, then... why aren't you winning more?

Now to the agents who have aligned with me, and those that are considering doing so, we have plans in the works that are about unbeatable. How powerful would it be for you, if when you are at your next listing appointment, to be able to guarantee that you could sell a home within a certain amount of days. How, you may ask? It's because if the house doesn't sell within the time frame you set, we will buy the home at a pre-listed price! How would that set you apart from the thousand other agents in the area?

As I've said over and over, in many different ways, I work for my agents and want to give them so many services and tools that no one in the area can compete against them. That's the Ramos way.

There's nothing wrong with making a living. But there's everything right in creating generational wealth.

CHAPTER 11

EXPANSION

In just about every industry, company owners want to expand. They want more — more locations, more products to sell, more services, more this, and more that. The reason, of course, is to make more money.

If someone starts a jazzy new restaurant that starts making money, the first thing they think is, *If I'm making this much money in this location, I bet I could double it in that location.* If they have the ability to act on their vision and their second location becomes successful, the next words out of their mouth are, *I bet I could franchise!*

We live in a society where we're judged by more. Basketball player Lebron James, for all of his accolades, will not be remembered as the best ever because Michael Jordan has more championships. Whether it's right or not, we value more. Nowadays when people pitch a movie to studio executives, they need to have the idea for the sequel in case it's a big hit. That's because the studio executives, like everyone else, want more.

In business more than in any other part of life more is king.

If someone has a record-breaking year, they raise their goals the following year so they can break the new record. More. More. More. We all want more.

Real estate agents want more as well. The problem is, it's not that easy. They've worked long and hard for many years to cultivate an area that supports them. Being a good agent requires skill and tenacity. You have to be willing to get up early, work late, and sacrifice your weekends in order to succeed. You have to be a good networker, know how to deal with people — which I refer to as knowing how to flex for different personality types — and know how to build solid relationships with people in the mortgage and banking industry, as well as with designers, inspectors, and the list goes on and on. You also have to have the patience of a saint to drive clients from home to home, and even after showing clients exactly what they asked for, drive them to another five homes. (If you're an agent right now, you're probably smirking because you've been there.)

There are many agents who have been in this industry far longer than I have, which is a true testament to their know-how and value. They've been through the ups and downs and have survived the infamous crash, but still, decades later, they're going strong. To get them to think about expanding into other regions is like asking them to do it all over again and it's a hard feat to duplicate. Most agents are taught to start small. If you have $1,000 to spend on flyers, the best use of that investment is not to blow it all in one blanket marketing blast, but to decrease the quantity of addresses and send those flyers to the same homes five or six times. So I understand when agents say expanding is not easy. That is why I'm not suggesting it for everybody. But it is possible. Actually, it's not only possible, but worth it!

Let's consider the clientele of people that move to the Tampa Bay area, which includes Clearwater, St. Petersburg, and other smaller towns. Half of them know where they want to move to. Perhaps they're snowbirds and have been vacationing here year after year, or perhaps they're moving here because of a job relocation so where the company is located dictates where they will move to, or perhaps they have friends and family and want to live close by, or perhaps they've done some research and love the schools, shopping, biking trails, golf courses, or proximity to the beach. For whatever reason they might have, only about 50 percent of people that move into this area know where they want to move to.

The other half has no idea. They just want to come to the Sunshine State. They see the Tampa Bay area as a growing market and want to live someplace near many beaches and close enough to Disney World. People don't need to know you in Oldsmar, Palm Harbor, South Tampa, or West Chase to get clients that you can move to Oldsmar, Palm Harbor, South Tampa, or West Chase. If you're their agent, they'll seriously consider your recommendation.

The first thing a couple in Chicago will do is a Google search for a Realtor® in a specific area. If your name is associated with multiple locations, you have a better chance of that couple contacting you. Sure, it's not as easy as all that except for... part of it is. The hard part is taking the leap of faith, of investing in perhaps another person at another location. But if you're successful now, it's because your model, strategy, and tactics are sound. It might take a while but it will end up being a good investment of your time, money, and energy. Keep marketing to the new area and you'll get a new listing that you'll convert to a sale. Once you get that first sale in a new market, you know the drill. Start ripping out those "recently sold" cards and you're up and running.

SCALE AND SCOPE

As an agent interested in expanding, I think you should first consider scale and scope. Scale means the geography you cover. Scope means the degree of services you offer. Let's discuss the geography you cover. Most agents get their business where they live. It's the foundation of their business. It's where their friends are, where they meet their kids' friends parents at birthday parties, where they congregate at their church, and where they do their extracurricular activities.

I'm no different. My grandparents lived in West Tampa, but my father moved us to South Tampa before I was born, so my roots were there. When I started developing new homes, I focused on South Tampa, specifically, a small island neighborhood called Davis Islands. I saw it to be the fastest growing, most desirable place to live in South Tampa. It was a great place to start because it was small enough for me to pour all my focus. When I opened my brokerage, I opened it in South Tampa, because that's what you do. You start where you're most comfortable, that's what you do. But once you start having great success, you expand.

Another way to expand is by scope, the services you offer. That's tough for the agent whose mentality is centered strictly on activities for buying and selling. By capitalizing on the many other transactions that occur when someone buys or sells a home, an agent can expand their services. It's important to study the different services you offer. Once you're confident and efficient at it, repeat the process over and over.

But, there can be more. If you've achieved a level of success with your model, strategy, and tactics in a geographical territory, trust that it could work in another. If you've built a team, maybe one or two people are on your payroll and the others are those you refer business to, and you're looking to add another team member, why not put that person in a different location?

Right now, agents associated with my brokerage can say they specialize in Hillsborough or Pinellas County. In essence, we have set up the first and most difficult step of expansion for the agents — an office. While they have one office that they prefer to work out of, their "home office," they can use any of the other three locations. The same goes for the construction products and referral network via Dakota, as well as our branding, web, and social media services with Organistics. They can even conduct events in our showroom or meet prospects at the Indigo Coffee House and Social Bar. My agents have the opportunity to take full advantage of all the offerings under the Ramos family of companies.

If I've explained myself correctly, the wheels in your head are churning right now. If 100 percent of your business is coming from one market and you are rock solid there, consider expanding. The people that know and trust you where you live won't abandon you. Enlarge your territory.

Now, don't do anything rash. As I said, expansion isn't for everyone. I think the agents who should seriously consider it are those whose brokers can support them. Sit with your broker and discuss your plans. See if, together, you can come to a resolution where you can serve another market and he or she can support you. That's the only way to truly grow, working hand in hand with your broker for the same goals.

Many people make forecasts. They'll write down the financial number they want to reach in a sticky note and attach it to their bathroom wall or their refrigerator. Some will go as far as to create a vision board and put it there. I'm a big believer in goal setting, so these practices are fine with me. In fact, I encourage every agent to continue to sign up for classes, learn more about the industry, and do whatever motivates them. However, regardless of how you motivate yourself, if you think you're going to do better financially by doing the same thing, you're fooling yourself. After all, the definition of insanity is doing the same things over and over but expecting a different result. To see real change in your finances, I believe you should leverage all of the learning you've done and the motivation you have and empower yourself to step out of your comfort zone. You're more capable than you know.

THE FUTURE OF RE/MAX BAY TO BAY

I'm going to continue to expand. There are many more clients I know we can serve. I have four locations now, but more are coming, whether through acquisition or partnerships. Currently I'm looking at the Clearwater Beach and St. Petersburg areas. After all, the name of my RE/MAX brokerage is "Bay to Bay." As I expand, the reach of the agents who work with me potentially expands. It is my goal to cover all points in the Tampa Bay Area. Imagine the Google rank you could achieve being listed in multiple locations. Right now it's four, but before long it will be more, with potentially more coming. Agents listed in multiple locations have a much bigger online presence than those listed in only one.

I'm also going to continue to expand the services we provide our agents, by way of creating them or through partnerships. Agents simply don't have the time to focus on every little moving piece, but the consumers are asking for them. It's the broker's job to stay ahead of the curve and help the agent stand out in a crowded marketplace. Another reason why I want to give them more services is because I too crave more.

IN CLOSING...

I wrote this book for three particular groups — agents, professionals who would like to be a real estate agent, and brokers. I'll address the brokers first.

There's a new wave coming. The Information Age can catapult your business or hinder it. You need to know how to harness it. Always be mindful that your clients are your agents. You work for them, not the other way around. They need to be given the tools, many more tools than what we were taught in brokerage school, to succeed. The more services and office concepts you can provide, the better you'll be able to recruit and retain agents.

I'd also like to extend an olive branch to RE/MAX brokers. I currently mentor some brokers and with humility, offer you the same. I always make myself available for collaboration and exploring synergistic opportunities. There's a way for us to help one another. I'm a phone call away.

To the professional who is considering becoming a real estate agent, I'll tell you that it's not easy. Going from a secure paycheck to a commission-based job is not for everybody. But it's well worth it!

If you've achieved a level of success in another field, there's no reason why you won't find success in real estate. I recommend you do an internal review and identify your competencies and skill sets and have confidence in yourself. Your success, especially in the beginning, depends greatly on the brokerage and partners you align yourself with. So do your due diligence, but don't wait forever. Once you've made the decision in your heart and mind, make the move. The world of real estate really is wonderful and it brings with it a myriad of other opportunities.

Lastly, to my fellow agents, I think it would behoove you to do this small exercise. Examine the last five clients you've helped and write down, if you can remember them all, every transaction they requested from your first conversation with them to your last. Then build a team who can handle those transactions to make the transitions smoother. If you want your next clients to refer you to the people they know, you have to knock their socks off.

It's acceptable to ask your broker for the support you believe you need, but at the end of the day, you wanted to be an agent because you wanted the onus on you. Well, it's on you. If you're not happy where you are, you have the power to make a change. Be true to yourself. Life is too short and your time is too valuable to waste.

Yes, I've built the four locations, but they are only successful because Zoe Green runs the brokerage with a steady hand and because of the talented agents who work there. We've recruited people with the same ethics, moral code, and culture we believe in. I'm fortunate to have such experienced go-getters who want to be ultra successful. Their results have amazed and humbled me. The ingenuity and tenacity of some of the agents possess inspires me.

Because of the synergy and culture we have all cultivated, I have seen agents who have only been in business for a year or two double their earnings. But that's what happens when you attract a team of talented, resourceful people who are, first and foremost, good people who are willing to share tips and help each other out. I'm fortunate to have so many gifted professionals aligned with me and I hope that more like-minded individuals would consider Ramos in the near future.

I try to manage my business the way the owner of a professional baseball franchise would manage a big-league team. I have a diverse team with varying degrees of success and experience, as one would have future hall of famers, home run hitters, and players just breaking into the minor leagues. While they all need some level of coaching and leadership, some need more than others.

However, they all need amenities and services that help expand their scale and scope — geography and services. If you're a home run hitter, is the coach asking you to lay down bunts, or is he allowing you to swing for the fences? Observe the field you play on, examine the amenities and ask yourself if it helps you. Do you play in an updated facility, complete with a state-of-the-art training room? When was the last time your office has been improved, either through new technology or a fresher, more streamlined process?

If you're not satisfied, the good news is that you don't have to call your agent and demand a trade. All you have to do is look around and see what other teams are doing. Get with a professional organization that offers everything you need to succeed. Life is too short and you have too much more to do.

The future of brokerages is here. Its foundations have been laid in the Tampa Bay area. It's built on service, information, collaboration, integrity, great products, and forward thinking. If you would like to know more, you are welcome to meet me at the Indigo Coffee shop in downtown Tampa or one of the three other locations I've built.

If I had it my way, you'd meet me where I'm from, South Tampa. That way, you don't have to go by what I say; you can go by what you see.

ACKNOWLEDGEMENTS

If I have achieved any level of success, it's not by coincidence. I've had help. I have been fortunate to share life experiences with many people that have become a part of my DNA, my backbone, and part of the fabric that makes me who I am. In addition to my wife Connie and my mother Mary Jane, whom I dedicate this book to; I have many other people I'd like to thank.

Wilfred Ramos – my father
Dad, you remain my best friend and hero. I have never met a man with as much vigor to live out his passions and who had the integrity living life the right way. The lessons and means by which you taught my brothers and I are unforgettable, utterly timeless. Above all, you taught me how to love, have compassion for people, and to follow my dreams. Although you left us in 2004, there is not a day that goes by where I don't feel you by my side. You have instilled in me the greatest gift you could – inspiration. I only hope that I give to my children what you've poured into me. You were a great father to me. You are my foundation.

Jeff Vardo – my high school baseball coach
You were the first person outside of my home that taught me the impact of great leadership. You took a bunch of scrappers and got the very best out of us and molded us into champions. Winning the Florida Baseball State Championship in 1988 and ending up as runners-up my senior year at H. B. Plant High are moments I'll always treasure. I've had a number of great coaches after graduating high school, some were in sports and others in business, and I've learned from each of them. But no one ever held a candle to what you did for our team and our individual pride. At the time, I didn't have the life experience to fully grasp the amazing job you did. I do now. You made a group of kids believe in themselves in a way that we never imagined. The friendships you've helped us cultivate and the memories we've created are a tribute to your impact on us. Thank you for teaching me how to compete, it has served me well.

Win Gurney, Jay Contessa, Brian Lernihan, and Greg Demetros – my mentors at Unilever
Collectively, as my managers at Unilever, you gave me the toughest tough love as a professional in corporate America. The lessons you taught me were unique to your own personalities and styles. Some of them were funny, others were exhilarating, excruciating, and a few were flat-out humiliating. But as I worked at Unilever from 1997 – 2004 and moved to five different cities, you've all taught me so much. I'd like to thank you each for going the extra mile with me and taking your valuable time in teaching me what a culture should be. The culture you created for me was fantastic, even in the midst of constant change. Thank you brothers!

Zoe Green – The real leader of my brokerage

You're more than my business partner and friend, you're the sister I never had. I could never have imagined the levels that we've achieved over the last 5 years. Despite all of the successes though, what I value most is our friendship because it revolves around serving our people and providing for our families. I appreciate the trust we have, where nothing is too petty to share. You are a gem and I want to thank you for being you and then for allowing me to be the best I could be. I could not have done this without you being my rock.

Eli Gonzalez – TG Publishing

Lastly, I'd like to acknowledge Eli Gonzalez for the time and diligence you've provided me in gathering my thoughts, conducting interviews, and helping me put my thoughts in a logical fashion. If it weren't for you, this book would have been 2,000 pages long! You are truly gifted at what you do. Also to Nathan Rodriguez for the illustrations – you're going to go far young man! And to Joe Wisinki for the great job of editing this book. Thank you!

ABOUT THE AUTHOR

James Ramos was born in Tampa, Florida. He graduated with a degree in Economics from the University of Florida and an MBA from Emory's Goizueta Business School. James is the youngest of 5 boys.

He began his career as an analyst with General Mills and worked in the Consumer Packaged Goods industry for 18 years, with other globally-recognized companies, Unilever and PepsiCo. He has worked in a broad range of roles: sales, marketing, finance, and product development. Having the opportunity to work on some of America's leading consumer brands, he learned to develop winning teams, create great product, and offer award winning service.

James moved back to Tampa in 2004, to follow his passion - real estate development, as his family has been in the construction business in Tampa since 1956. Since that time, he has added integral divisions to his construction roots: development, real estate, design, and finance. Most recently, he returned to the food and beverage industry when he bought a coffee brand.

James believes in being a servant leader and devotes his time to the recruitment and retention of key members that hold the same passion and integrity the Ramos Family is known for.

His main office is located in South Tampa with 3 other locations across 2 counties with over 100 full time professionals focused around 6 key areas of development: FINANCE, BUY, SELL, DESIGN, BUILD, and FURNISH.

Today he lives with his loving and supportive wife and their two children, and dedicates his time building relationships throughout the Tampa Bay area. Ramos' philanthropic involvement is broad, raising awareness for Primary Immunodeficiencies (PI) with the Jeffrey Modell Foundation, All Children's Hospital, and the University of South Florida's Department of Pediatrics. Ramos was an executive board member responsible for development at the Glazer Children's Museum in downtown Tampa.

When James is not working one of his many businesses, he likes to spend time with his family. He also enjoys cooking. He lives an active lifestyle and likes to work out, bike, and swim. He considers being at the beach and spending time in Park City - skiing to be his two places of sanctuary.

To read more about James Ramos visit:

www.jamesramos.com

SOURCES

1 — Ch. 1
Source for billionaires:
Carlyle, Erin. "Meet the 20 Richest Real Estate
Billionaires." Wikipedia. Accessed December 07, 2016.
https://en.wikipedia.org/wiki/Forbes_list_of_billionaires.

2. — Ch. 2
https://www.nar.realtor/sites/default/files/
policies/2017/2017-Code-of-Ethics.pdf

3 — Ch. 2
"Field Guide to Quick Real Estate Statistics." https://www.
nar.realtor/field-guides/field-guide-to-quick-real-estate-
statistics.

4. — Ch. 2
McChrystal, Stan. "Lessons from Iraq It Takes a Network
to Defeat a Network." https://www.linkedin.com/
pulse/20130621110027-86145090-lesson-from-iraq-it-
takes-a-network-to-defeat-a-network.

5. — Ch. 2
https://www.thebalance.com/real-estate-agents-and-
realtors-1798898